From Joe & Irene

The Story of Lighthouses

BOOKS BY MARY ELLEN CHASE

A Goodly Heritage · *Mary Peters*
Silas Crockett · *Dawn in Lyonesse*
A Goodly Fellowship · *Windswept*
Jonathan Fisher: Maine Parson
The Bible and the Common Reader
The Plum Tree · *The White Gate*
Life and Language in the Old Testament
The Edge of Darkness · *The Lovely Ambition*
The Psalms for the Common Reader
The Prophets for the Common Reader
Victoria: A Pig in a Pram
Richard Mansfield, the Prince of Donkeys
Dolly Moses, the Cat and the Clam Chowder
A Journey to Boston

The Story of
LIGHTHOUSES

by Mary Ellen Chase

Wood Engravings by Erwin Schachner

W · W · NORTON & COMPANY · INC · NEW YORK

This book is dedicated with love to my niece
BARBARA CHASE
who all her life has known and loved
lighthouses.

ACKNOWLEDGMENTS

I wish to thank Emma Kaplan of the Smith College Library for her great help in procuring books for me which have to do with lighthouses, and Nicholas Chrisman for sharing with me his own knowledge of the Pharos of Alexandria.

M.E.C.

Contents

AN IMPORTANT LETTER
TO THE READERS OF THIS BOOK

Dear Reader:

I want to tell you what this book will be about.

Although it is called in its title a story, it must be a history as well. To be sure, it will tell many stories of danger and of almost incredible devotion, many of which come from my own experience, for I have had a great deal to do with lighthouses in my life. Yet it must be also, and in a very real sense, a history, and a history of lighthouses in other countries than our own; for although our lighthouses have stood on our islands and headlands for more than two hundred years, they all received their being from the lighthouses of other lands than ours, from Egypt, and the Roman Empire, and England. Any story of our lighthouses would be entirely incomplete unless we learned first of the fabulous Pharos of Alexandria, the Roman lights, and the great Eddystone towers.

There is yet another sense in which this book must be a history. For lighthouses, their brave keepers and the boys and girls who were brought up on lonely, seaswept rocks and reefs and on isolated islands, really belong to the past rather than to the present. In this new age of mechanical devices and of electronics, more and more lighthouses are manned by machinery rather than by men. This stupendous change, moving always on and on, is without any doubt right and wise; and yet it is bound often to sacrifice human interest to wisdom.

Since the year 1939 the lighthouses of the United States, for many years under the Lighthouse Service, have been placed in the excellent care of the United States Coast Guard, of stalwart young men who can bear loneliness, since they are awarded frequent leaves from duty, and since they now have not only radio, but television

14

to make their long evenings less long. The former keepers of the lights, after giving most of their lives to the constant tending of great lamps and lanterns, no longer must climb numberless stairs every four hours all night to be sure that their lights always stream forth in the darkness and through the storms.

Most of such gallant men are now dead. Yet they have become indispensable, even noble figures in the history of our country. It would be a pity for us not to know about them and to accord them the honor which they deserve as richly as do the more familiar figures of our Presidents, our great generals and admirals, our leading statesmen and educators.

Therefore, this book which you are beginning to read will be both history and story; and it cannot fail to be interesting because it will deal with human courage, with selfless devotion to one's job in life, with unbelievable feats of engineering—in brief, with the battle of the hands and the minds against gigantic, sweeping seas, against snow and fog, wind and ice, against all those mighty forces of Nature which have been with us since the world began. And, as I have said before, it will be a history also of early lighthouses, which many centuries ago reared their massive towers, not in America but far away, and which by the skill of their builders taught

15

many and helpful things to our later and better-trained engineers and architects.

For reasons of space this book will not contain any account of those other necessary aids to sailors, with lightships like the famous ones on the perilous Nantucket Shoals and on the Ambrose Channel reefs at the entrance to New York harbor. It will not deal with the lighthouses on our Great Lakes. Nor will it include those thousands of beacons and buoys which ensure the safety of ships from the coast of Maine to the Panama Canal, from the Mississippi River and the Thames to the countless ports of the Mediterranean Sea.

Its thrilling subject is limited to ocean lighthouses, old and at least relatively new, ancient and modern, lighthouses from Egypt to the cruel ledges of Maine, from the great Eddystone Light off England, most famous of all lighthouses in the world, to that lonely and desolate rock, Tillamook, which receives the full sweep of the Pacific at its worst off the coast of Oregon.

So—let us begin—in the hope that all who read these pages will be filled with pride in human endurance and sacrifice and thrilled by the knowledge of what men and boys, and women and girls, too, have done both to make the seas safe for ships and sailors and to make their own lives of value and of meaning to the larger life of the world—a life which includes the whole great family of humanity and to which we all owe our devotion and our service, whatever that service may be.

Yours, for good books and good reading,
Mary Ellen Chase

Northampton, Massachusetts
April, 1965

❖ I ❖

The Oldest Lighthouse in
the World

BEFORE WE BEGIN TO READ ABOUT THE VERY OLD-
est lighthouse of which we have reliable record, we
should remember, of course, that Nature herself built
the first lighthouses. Countless ages before man inhabited
the earth and long centuries before he had begun to feel
any responsibility for his fellowmen who sailed the seas,
or anxious even over the fate of those material necessities
brought to him by ships, Nature had framed mountains
which, like Mt. Etna and Mt. Vesuvius, sent forth smoke
by day and, often, flames of fire both in daylight and

in darkness. Volcanoes were without doubt the earliest lighthouses.

There were other landmarks, too, provided by Nature to be of help to all early mariners, who possessed few means of navigation beyond a rude compass and various crude devices for sounding the depths of water. Familiar hills and cliffs were of indispensable assistance to sailors, as were tall trees or an isolated clump of trees. So valuable, indeed, were trees held as signs to seafarers that in the sixteenth century in England a law was passed which imposed a heavy fine on anyone ruining the outline of a group of trees or cutting down one of especial height, provided such trees grew above the sea. This law of 1566 stated explicitly that by the destruction of such marks men and ships had been "miscarried or lost." Even so important a personage as the Bishop of Winchester was accused by the seventeenth-century diarist, Samuel Pepys, of felling trees which for years had been of utmost importance to ships approaching the harbor of Portsmouth. The angry diarist actually reported that esteemed cleric to the King of England, on the claim that he might well be causing disaster to ships, and death to those who sailed them!

Thus men were but following upon Nature's good example when they began to think about ensuring the safety of ships and sailors. In the earlier ages of civilization they built beacon fires upon high places, at first probably for the sending of messages or for the celebration of great events, but afterward surely for the help of ships at sea. In Europe in the Middle Ages it became the custom to place lanterns in church towers or candles in the sea-facing windows of houses built upon headlands. Monks and nuns in early monastic enclosures seem to have been aware of the aid which *they* might offer by keeping lights burning at night if their buildings were located near the ocean. There are even records of hermits living in medieval lighthouses and themselves acting as lightkeepers between their fastings and their prayers. Perhaps it was this identification of lights with religion which led to the custom of the placing of chapels in early English and European lighthouses. For several, if not many, had such chapels in their towers.

2

The oldest man-made lighthouse of which we have any accurate history was the famous Pharos of Alexandria in Egypt, named among the Seven Wonders of the World. And it surely was a wonder, not only to its ancient day, but to all later times and places! Its tower rose more than four hundred feet in height from an island called Pharos at the western entrance to the harbor of Alexandria, an island surrounded then by dangerous reefs and shoals, now a peninsula and a part of the mainland of Egypt. The tower is said to have been built of hewn blocks of white limestone and decorated by marble even whiter; and it was so famed far and wide throughout the third century B.C., and in every land of its day, that Pharos, the name of its island, came to be given to all succeeding lighthouses wherever they were built.

This ancient lighthouse belonged to the vast empire of a young man known to history as Alexander the Great. Alexander came from the Province of Macedonia in the northern part of the peninsula of Greece. He was born there in 356 B.C. While he was still in his twenties, through a series of brilliant military conquests, he made himself master of most of the world of his day. A legend tells us that, when he realized there were no more countries for him to conquer, he burst into tears! Another legend, and a far more pleasant one, says that he became so much in love with the poetry of Homer, which he learned from a famous tutor of his boyhood, that he always slept with a copy of the *Iliad* under his pillow wherever he might be.

There is more than a little sadness in the knowledge

that young Alexander himself never lived to see and to admire the great Pharos, the glory of the city which he had built and to which he had given his name. He died when he was only thirty-three years old of a fever in Babylon in the year 323 B.C. He would have felt a consuming interest in that first of lighthouses; for his tutor, who was none other than the renowned Greek philosopher, Aristotle, was a man who knew not only philosophy, but mathematics, other sciences of his time, and a great deal about natural history. He was fascinated by the weather, the planets, the earth, and the sea; and it is surely most likely that, in the seven years which he spent with Alexander, he should have inspired his pupil with his own enthusiasms and delights.

Young Alexander, who died a year before his famous teacher died, would have loved the Pharos and taken great pride in every detail of its amazing construction. Its architect was a Greek named Sostratus from the town of Cnidus in Asia Minor. We know all too little about him; yet he must have been not only one of the leading mathematicians and scientists of his day, but a man of daring and adventure as well. He began his work on the Pharos around 300 B.C. and finished it twenty years later. As patrons of his remarkable triumph of ancient engineering, he had, instead of Alexander, two kings of

Egypt, who, as generals of Alexander, followed him as rulers in Egypt and who were known as the Ptolemies. Ptolemy Soter saw the beginning of the great lighthouse, and Ptolemy Philadelphus, his son, its completion.

In their capital city of Alexandria, which, we are told, boasted of four thousand palaces, four thousand public baths, four hundred theaters and other places of popular amusement, as many as twelve thousand gardens, and a vast library, the pride of the ancient world, no marvel equaled the Pharos rising from its rocky island. Poets and scientists—and Alexandria was proud in the possession of both—united in their wonder at it, for it appealed to the sense of beauty as well as to that of architectural and engineering genius. Just as the Parthenon two centuries earlier had become inseparably identified with Athens, so the Pharos became Alexandria, and Alexandria became the Pharos. It fired the imagination of men as well as shed its light upon the sea; and that light which it kindled in ancient minds was to endure in the memory of the world centuries after its actual light had been extinguished.

Travelers came to see it from every land under the sun. Famous men wrote about it. Julius Caesar, who saw it in 48 B.C., was overwhelmed by its superb construction. Twenty years later the Greek geographer,

Strabo, described it with awe, praising the pure whiteness of its stonework decorated with the whitest of marble. In A.D. 77, two years before his cruel death in the eruption of Mt. Vesuvius, the Roman historian, Pliny the Elder, wrote about it in his *Natural History*, extolling its age, which was then three hundred and fifty years, and comparing it with the later lighthouses of the Roman Empire. Pliny, perhaps curiously, saw possible danger in it as well as safety, since he expresses fear lest in the darkness of the night its glow may be mistaken by navigators for a star in the sky!

What, so far as we can learn from dependable records, was the Pharos of Alexandria really like? In terms of dimension, its huge base and its lofty height, it must have been the largest lighthouse ever to be built in any age. Its mighty base was one hundred feet square and contained three hundred rooms for the men who worked at its building and for those who would later tend and guard its light. Three stories rose above this mammoth base, two of them filled by a spiral ascent or by a steep, winding staircase, the third given to its lantern. And at the very top, standing on the great lantern itself, was a statue of Poseidon, god of the seas.

The entrance to the Pharos must have been impressive, even magnificent. The lighthouse stood in a vast court, which was entered between tall columns of white marble. More columns rose about the tower itself; and the court was kept green and beautiful by gardens and trees.

How was this masterpiece of ancient engineering lighted? That, of course, is the chief question; and it is difficult to answer with any assurance of unquestionable truth. In all probability wood fires burned on its top, fires doubtless sheltered from wind and rain by some form of metal covering. Pliny's description surely suggests such fires, which he says are "uninterrupted" in their burning. We know that fires of wood or of coal were used in many lighthouses of Europe as late as the mid-nineteenth century. They seem to have been the natural inheritance of beacon fires; and in times of cheap, or costless labor, which in the case of Alexandria was performed by slaves, the constant carrying of fuel to the summit of the lighthouse would not have seemed an insuperable task.

We cannot be entirely sure, however, that the Pharos was lighted at night by a fire blazing from its lantern and sending forth warning wreaths of smoke by day. Persistent tradition, probably born of the remarkable scientific knowledge and research of ancient Alexandria, claims that it carried also on its summit a "mirror," which was held to be even more wonderful than the tower itself and which by means of reflectors threw the light by night and the rays of the sun by day far across the sea. It is not impossible, of course, that some famous scientists of the learned city had discovered the power of the *lens* and that their discovery was lost and forgotten when the Pharos fell, only to be rediscovered long centuries later.

This first and greatest of lighthouses, however it was lighted, kept on with its work for ships and sailors for more than seven centuries. Its lantern was destroyed in the Arab Conquest of Egypt, which began in the autumn of A.D. 641; and although restorations were begun by later Arab rulers, the great light never again streamed forth from its lofty tower. About A.D. 1100 and again some three centuries afterward two severe earthquakes finally put an end to this wonder of the ancient world. Its ruins today form part of an Egyptian mosque and fort. The *National Geographic* has recently given hope that more of its actual ruins may soon be discovered and certified beyond a doubt.

Nevertheless, gone though the Pharos is, the magic of its name perseveres, bright and shining like its high, mysterious lantern. Lighthouses have always possessed a singular romance; and this oldest of them all still holds and will always hold power to fill us with interest and curiosity. Like young Alexander the Great, who was denied its wondrous sight by his too early death, we have missed our sight of it, even in true pictures, because of the centuries of time. Yet in our imaginations it can still glow. For it was one of the triumphs of the mind of man which is ageless, and which is forevermore the priceless treasure of us all.

✤ II ✤

The Lighthouses of the Roman Empire

THE ROMANS WERE NOT IN ANY SENSE AN IMAGI-
native people. They were, instead, practical, hard-
headed, and definite, plain-spoken, frank, even boastful.
They liked to *do* things; and they were justly proud of
the work of their able and skillful hands. As we all know,
they have left in the many lands which they conquered
in the first four hundred years of the Christian era, when
their Empire controlled the world of its day, many proofs
of their genius at architecture and engineering: the
wonderful roads which they made, like the Great North

33

Road leading from London; great bridges like those at Auxerre and Avignon in France, which they called Gaul; theaters like the one at Arles; walls like those at Colchester in England; aqueducts, baths, mosaic pavements, and various devices for heating the rooms of their great, cold houses. They took vast pride in all their works. Why, then, did they not leave more proofs of their skill in building lighthouses?

For they surely *did* build lighthouses. These they needed for their many ships and sailors who carried Roman goods far beyond the Mediterranean to the lonely outposts of their Empire and brought back all sorts of wares from their many provinces. The description of a dinner, given by a wealthy Roman in the second century, tells of wine, mushrooms, and other delicacies which had been brought by his ships from faraway countries in order both to please and to impress his guests.

Lighthouses, then, were most certainly a necessity to Roman navigation; and history, or at least stout tradition, claims that the Romans erected no less than thirty of them, from the shores of the Black Sea to those of the Atlantic Ocean. Yet we are curiously in want of thoroughly reliable facts about most of these helps to Roman mariners.

We do know, however, that two early lighthouses were constructed on the cliffs of Boulogne in France and of Dover in England, which was, of course, the Roman province of Britain. The practical Roman mind evidently seized upon the height of these rocky eminences which meant that the light-bearing towers themselves need not be so high and, hence, so costly to build. Only eighty feet of actual building was necessary in each case in order to obtain towers which rose nearly four hundred feet above the sea.

Suetonius, that Roman historian who is perhaps more fascinating than he is always accurate, assures us that the Emperor Caligula, whom Suetonius quite truly calls "a monster of vice," built such lighthouses on these cliffs, only twenty miles apart across the English Channel, about the year A.D. 40. A Roman medal cast about A.D. 185 clearly pictures the Boulogne tower, which Charlemagne restored in A.D. 811; and there is not much question as to the existence of that at Dover, where Roman remains have been visible up to fairly recent times. In fact, those two lighthouses were probably the first erected in Western Europe after its conquest by the Roman legions.

There is excellent authority also for believing that the Romans built a lighthouse at Messina in Sicily, which perhaps was helped now and again by the flames from nearby Mt. Etna, and another at Ravenna, that resident city of the later Roman emperors in northern Italy on the Adriatic Sea. Ravenna was a city renowned in the fourth century for its trade. In its spacious harbor two hundred and fifty ships could ride at anchor; and surely for their safe arrival and departure a lighthouse was needed. Pliny the Elder, again in his *Natural History,* says that "a light burned brightly" at Ravenna even in his much earlier day.

The biggest and the best lighthouse built by Roman architects and engineers was certainly that at Ostia, the harbor at the mouth of the River Tiber. Pliny the Elder assures us of that fact; and since Pliny died in A.D. 79, the lighthouse must have been built in early imperial days, when Ostia became important as the port of Rome. Its date is given as around A.D. 50 in the reign of Claudius, the fourth Emperor of Rome.

After the Roman engineers had dredged out and built the harbor of Ostia, they placed a lighthouse on an artificial island, made for that purpose between two long breakwaters which marked the harbor entrance. Suetonius also stresses the fact that a lighthouse was there "to guide the course of ships"; and he even compares its lofty tower to the Pharos of Alexandria, although it was actually only one-quarter the height of the Pharos. The Emperor Claudius saw to it that a huge statue of himself stood before its tower in the best imperial tradition; and although this lighthouse at Ostia was never numbered among the wonders of the world, it clearly seemed wonderful to the Roman historians who took the trouble to write about it.

A certain Roman lady, elderly and quite unknown, has helped at least a little to dispel the mystery of Roman lighthouses through the chance discovery of her tombstone. Her name was Firma Victora. Either she, or members of her family, or her friends who knew how she liked lighthouses, or perhaps how she herself symbolized their helpful light, caused one to be carved upon her tombstone. Firma Victora's lighthouse even suggested in its sculpture the flames of fire blazing from its summit! So—in her death—she has not only helped to establish the fact of Roman lighthouses, but she has also told us how they sent forth their light to aid slaves toiling at the oars of Roman galleys.

❖ III ❖

The Most Famous

of All Lighthouses

THE ANCIENT PHAROS OF ALEXANDRIA WAS WITH-
out doubt the most *fabulous* of all lighthouses of any age.
But it has never been considered the most *famous*. After
all, its skillful architect and his unknown workmen had
an island to build it on. They did not have to labor on
treacherous ledges at low tide, ledges even then often
swept by mountainous and malignant waves. Their tower
did have a sure foundation from the beginning. They
were not constantly drenched to the skin at all hours of
work and quite reasonably scared *out* of their skins as

well. So—let us grant that the Pharos was fabulous beyond words, deservedly one of the Seven Wonders of the World, and yet at the same time understand that it has never been held to be the most famous of lighthouses.

Of course, there are many famous lighthouses which have become household words, even if those who speak of them have never seen them. There is the great tower of Cape Hatteras, painted in striking black-and-white spiral bands and rising one hundred and ninety-three feet into the air, a tower originally built as early as 1798 and marking perhaps the most perilous region of our long Atlantic coastline. Hatteras and the nearby Diamond Shoals, together the veritable home of hurricanes and of mighty seas, had caused numberless disasters to ships before Alexander Hamilton in 1794 convinced the Senate of the young United States that a lighthouse there was a necessity. There is the Bell Rock Light eleven miles off the eastern coast of Scotland on the Inchcape Rock, which poets have celebrated. There is the famous lighthouse at the Lizard Point in Cornwall, the very idea of which was hated and deplored by greedy and wicked men who had for centuries profited by the wrecks of ships. Such men conceived diabolical schemes to entice ships to their doom. Nor did they hesitate to add murder to their crimes. They wanted no such aid to ships and sailors as a light at the Lizard would provide! There is the first American lighthouse built at Boston on Little Brewster Island as early as 1716 in colonial days. There is the incredible tower on Minot's Ledge which marks the hostile reefs off Cohasset. All these feats of stubborn engineering justly claim our pride; and yet they, one and all, yield their right to fame to the first lighthouse ever erected on what had seemed for centuries to be an uncontrollable, lonely, isolated mass of rock in the midst of unbelievable seas.

The most famous of all lighthouses, then, is the Eddystone Light; and its construction the most original, daring, and dramatic story in lighthouse history. Where is it? Why is it rightly accorded such distinction? How was its building almost miraculously accomplished? By whom? When? And at what awful cost?

2

The word Eddystone itself means *the stone of reeling waters.* No name could be more apt. It is, in fact, a perfect description. This stone, or shelf of cruel rock, is part of an underwater reef, some six hundred yards in length, which lies in the English Channel fourteen miles southwest of the important harbor of Plymouth.

This brutal reef had long been famous, or infamous, in English seafaring history, as we know from the many references made to it by English chroniclers. Hakluyt in his *Voyages*, published in the sixteenth century, writes of shipwrecks there as do less well-known chroniclers earlier than his day. One of them borrows a term from the Roman poet, Horace, to describe the Eddystone rocks. They are *scopulos infamis,* he says, "infamous, horrible rocks." To those brave English seamen and adventurers of the sixteenth century, men who like Sir Francis Drake gave to England much of her maritime distinction, the Eddystone threatened far more peril than the open sea. In order to reach the safety of Plymouth harbor they had to pass it, a terror which was always with them and especially on their homeward voyages.

There was another chronicler of the Eddystone reef who has meant a great deal to our own history. This was the captain of the ship *Mayflower,* which sailed from Plymouth in England on September 6, 1620, to land some two months later with the Pilgrim Fathers in another harbor to be also named Plymouth, or Plimouth. The captains of ships are not usually very fulsome and detailed in their logs; but this captain took time on September 6, 1620 to write about the Eddystone, which, he said, "we managed to avoid." He described it as "a wicked reef of twenty-three rust-red granite rocks . . . great ragged stones around which the sea constantly eddies, a grave danger to all ships hereabouts . . . and always to be dreaded by mariners."

Eddystone with its sharp pinnacles of red rock was not only in itself the most dangerous of reefs. Its danger was a hundredfold increased by its very situation and by the peculiar nature of the tides which washed it. In the first place, it was exposed to the full force of those prevailing westerly winds of the Atlantic which blow up seas bound to collide with those from the north sweeping down beyond the Straits of Dover and giving to the narrow English Channel its deserved reputation as one of the most difficult and menacing of seaways. And these chaotic seas were often made even more monstrous by the unusual turbulence of the Bay of Biscay, between Spain and France, whose strong tides and undertows were felt miles away in Channel waters. In the second place, English Channel tides have a distinctive nature of their own, by which their seething ebb and flow give the effect of four tides in twenty-four hours instead of the normal two. Because of this phenomenon, the Eddystone rocks seemed always dashed by waves, always to be a chaos of angry waters obedient to no law.

As Plymouth grew in importance until it became one of the best known and busiest seaports of England, so did the dread of the Eddystone rocks increase. For as more and more ships were sailing to and from Plymouth, ships from the new ports of America and the old ports of the Far East, the number of Eddystone victims was steadily rising to make a mockery of the superb harbor, its wealth, and its pride. In the late seventeenth century the idea of a lighthouse on that revengeful reef began to tease the minds of thousands of Englishmen, and not alone those of ship owners and of merchants who had lost fortunes through disaster, but those of ordinary people who could no longer bear the history and the present reality of suffering and cruel death. Fantastic as the notion seemed, weak as was the faith that the Eddystone could ever be conquered by the minds and the hands of men, the will and the desire constantly increased to slay this monster who had slain so many ships and sailors.

3

This Herculean labor of securing the base of a lighthouse upon an isolated reef swept by the full force of mighty seas, and afterward raising a tower upon it, had never before been undertaken. It meant at best inter-mittent toil, possible only at low tide, and, in the case of the Eddystone, entirely impossible for days on end be-cause of winds and seas which made landing on its rock completely out of the question. Needless to say, any work at all during the winter months was inconceivable.

It may be that a crude comparison, a simple dia-gram, will make more clear to those who are reading this book the appearance of the Eddystone reef and the tremendous obstacles which its very shape and features presented. Let me, then, suggest an easy way to make such a comparison. If you will extend far apart the mid-dle and the index finger of your left hand, together with your thumb, you will have an imperfect, but perhaps helpful picture of the red Eddystone rocks which rose above the sea in three ridges. The only one of the three which, because of its width, could safely support the foundation for a lighthouse was the central ridge, or, in our comparison, your index finger. Let your thumb stand for a line of more or less separate and jagged rocks rising sharply above the seas to the right, and your mid-dle finger for a narrower reef to the left and somewhat above the one in the center. Of these three ridges which together formed the dreaded shelves and pinnacles of rock, only this middle ridge, or, again, your index finger,

47

presented also, not far from its northern end, a sufficient surface above the ocean for the base and the tower of a lighthouse.

Rough and uneven though this exposed surface was, impossible as it seemed to land men and materials upon it, it nevertheless appealed to the vision and the daring of four singularly remarkable men, who, one after another, over the long space of two centuries, fought wind, waves, and weather to build four towers in succession to warn ships against these inhospitable and threatening ridges of rock. Perhaps the men themselves were, in personality, as singular and remarkable as was their work. Who were they?

Before I introduce them, one by one, and try to choose words to describe the disheartenments, triumphs, and tragedies which marked their almost insuperable achievements, I would remind my readers that civil engineering as we know it today was entirely unknown to seventeenth- and eighteenth-century England. Even in the late nineteenth century, when the fourth and final Eddystone lighthouse rose and when technology had made such mammoth strides that the work of the fourth builder was as nothing compared to that of his stubborn forerunners, formal training in civil and in marine engineering was still in its infancy. The four men who built their lighthouses on the Eddystone reef were not men disciplined in engineering as men are disciplined today. Instead, they were men who loved the mechanics of building, who were devoted to doing things with their hands, who scorned the idea of being beaten by mere forces of Nature, gigantic as such forces might be. They were men who welcomed the challenge of struggling against ferocious sea, against storm and fog and cold, in order to accomplish what to other men seemed chimerical and, indeed, impossible. They were very different as individuals, it is true; yet they all were fired by the same ambition.

4

Perhaps the builder of the first Eddystone tower was the most singular and unique of all the four pioneers. His name was Henry Winstanley. He came from Saffron Walden in Essex, a small and lovely English town which boasted on its outskirts a great house known as Audley End.

Audley End had been built in Elizabethan days by the first Earl of Suffolk, a county on the border of Essex; and it was held, in its original form, to outshine in splendor even the royal palace at Hampton Court. Today, although it has lost much of its size and magnificence, it is still visited by countless tourists, eager to see its Tudor architecture and its rich furnishings. In 1644, when Henry Winstanley was born, it had few rivals among the great houses of England. So renowned was it, indeed, as a palace that the third Earl of Suffolk sold it to King Charles II, who frequently transferred his court there and made it his home for long periods of time.

When Henry was born, his father was the caretaker and the accountant of Audley End; and by the time Henry was twenty-one, he became an assistant to his father. Always eager for prestige and publicity, Henry was only too happy to find himself not many years later a member of a king's household; and he saw to it that he became a companion as well as a servant to those who made up the royal entourage. Apparently because of his liveliness and originality, important people began to speak highly of him, although there seems to have been amusement as well as respect in their opinion of him. His mind was volatile as well as intelligent; he had somehow managed to travel widely in Europe; and he adored with an uncontrollable passion the unusual and the curious. He was, in fact, an incorrigible innovator and inventor. He may not have been exactly a crackpot;

but there was more than a little madness both in his behavior and in many of his ingenious contrivances. And he was always a poseur and an inveterate publicity-seeker.

The country girl from Saffron Walden whom Henry Winstanley married must have found life with him a series of excitements and surprises. The house which he built two miles from Audley End was, to say the least, unusual. A huge clock decorated one side of its front, and a barometer, the other side. Its roof was crowned with a large lantern, especially designed by Henry to throw light far and wide. In its garden stood a windmill which actually pumped water for household use.

Within doors Henry Winstanley's power of invention and his rather bizarre humor fully indulged themselves; for there he contrived all manner of devices to embarrass, disconcert, and even to frighten visitors. He used mirrors to make all kinds of illusory effects; and he specialized in trick chairs, one of which immediately enclosed within its suddenly moving arms anyone who sat in it and imprisoned its alarmed occupant until he cried out for rescue.

Nor was young Henry at all averse to making money from his various inventions. He blatantly advertised the contents of his home as *Winstanley's Wonders;* and so widely did these wonders become known that people from all parts of England, as far away, indeed, as Land's End, willingly paid a shilling to marvel at them and to be tricked by them. It was not long before a home in the country began to seem both too provincial and too little lucrative for so eminent an inventor. Henry's ambitions led him to London where, in the heart of that city, near Piccadilly, he designed and built a new place of amusement, which he called *Winstanley's Waterworkes*. Here he achieved "marvels" with fountains and waterspouts; and this London venture became most popular not only with the "masses," but with the nobility as well.

In his spare time he was never idle. His constant labor at one thing or another became as well-known as his flair for publicity. He made playing cards, designed and drawn to suit the different countries of the world; he made engravings on copper plates of the most celebrated English estates. By the time he had reached middle age he had become renowned not only as an eccentric, an artist, and a fabulous showman, but actually as a mechanical genius, indeed as one of the most inventive men of his day. Some people, it is said, had the boldness and the temerity to class him, in ability as well as in time, with Sir Christopher Wren, the great architect of St.

Paul's Cathedral and the gifted designer and builder of many smaller London churches. If such an absurd rating ever reached Henry Winstanley's greedy ears, how he would have rejoiced—he who always was careful to sign his name with the abbreviation *Gent.* attached to it! Nor did he omit to do this, even on his ill-fated lighthouse!

With the wealth which he had gained from his various enterprises, he launched around the age of fifty into another sort of business, one exceedingly profitable, but most risky. He bought five trading ships. When two of these had been lost on the Eddystone rocks, and he had lost thousands of English pounds through these disasters, he in his fury went himself to Plymouth to find out when something was to be done about a lighthouse to combat this frightful enemy of men and ships. He discovered what he already suspected, that, although the authority for a lighthouse had been given two years earlier, no builder could be found who was willing to undertake such a perilous and impossible task.

Whereupon in his anger, and in his anxiety over his loss, and bolstered up by his desire for fame and his unquenchable confidence in his own powers, he announced that he, Henry Winstanley, Gentleman, of Audley End and of London, would build a lighthouse on the hated Eddystone reef—by his own hands and with his own genius!

Winstanley began his lighthouse in the summer of 1696, after having spent the preceding winter in making plans for it, both mechanical and mental. He knew that his first job was somehow to anchor the base of his tower to that red, merciless rock; for this he determined to drive twelve iron rods into twelve deep holes and to fill the circle which they made with cement. The weather in July seemed designed to frustrate him. For days on end no boat could reach the reef; and even when it could, it often took four or five hours of heavy rowing from Plymouth. The most brawny of Devonshire and Cornwall men were tired out before they so much as arrived at the desolate scene of their monstrous labors.

It is only fair to their overseer to say that his workmen thoroughly liked, respected, and admired him. Mad though he doubtless was, or at least so odd that he seemed mad to them, he made himself one of them, as he swung his pickaxe into the stubborn red rock. He was always good-tempered, always reasonable, always brave. Like them all, he was drenched to the skin, and tied by stout ropes to the rocks against the ravenous waves. Like them all, he was ready to do the most menial work.

He bound them to him by his friendly understanding of the chimerical task they were all up against and by his never-failing optimism. They one and all pronounced him the best of companions. When a wave washed him in his turn into the sea, he either laughed or cursed; and he was a genius at cursing with utter abandon. One of the miracles of his lighthouse was his personality, his indomitable, hopeful disposition; and this fired them all to do their utmost for him. For three years he persevered with them until at last in 1698 they saw his tower rising from its seemingly strong and stable foundation.

Of course, since he was the sort of man he was, his lighthouse, which he enlarged and strengthened during the third year of its building, had many absurd features. Not realizing that the force of waves is greater against stones placed in the shape of a square than in that of a circle, he built much of his rather ridiculous tower, above its circular base, in the shape of a polygon, and, prompted by his perennial love of display, decorated it outside and inside with unnecessary additions and excrescences. One of these was a bedchamber, "richly gilded and painted," which he had constructed in the hope of royal, or at least of noble visitors. They never came. Another chamber just above was a Room of State, "well carved" and furnished "with ample cupboards," also for important but nonexistent visitors. Outside, there was a great deal of fretted ironwork and a massive weathervane on the top of the lantern. Needless to add, there was a Latin inscription above the main entrance door which proclaimed that this Pharos had been designed and constructed by Henry Winstanley, Gent. Winstanley saw that the *Gent.* was there even though the Latin had no word for it!

On November 14, 1698, Henry himself climbed up his many stairs to his lantern and lighted there a good number of tallow candles. Fishermen and those who sailed in bigger craft began to bless Henry Winstanley, though they one and all questioned whether his lighthouse could long endure the worst of Atlantic storms. Henry himself never questioned its endurance. To him it was there for keeps; and to any doubter he always responded with the hope that he might be in it through "the greatest storm that ever was."

He got his wish. On November 26, 1703, after his tower had lighted the sea for five years, he spent the night in his lighthouse. Following a fortnight of evil weather, the greatest storm that England has ever known in her long history burst upon her. Winstanley, then a man of fifty-nine, had gone out to his Eddystone creation to make repairs necessary after the recent gales. At midnight, after some strange and sinister hours of calm, a great wind blew up from the southwest, a tempest or a tornado, which not only blew, but screamed and thundered. All over southern England church spires toppled, great trees were uprooted, houses were reduced to rubble. Daniel Defoe could now add to his Great Plague and his Great Fire his description of the Great Storm. The loss of ships was well over a hundred; and many hundreds of sailors died that night on a score of unprotected reefs.

The Eddystone showed its light until midnight of November 26. By daybreak it had gone. No sign that it had ever existed remained save for a few broken rods of iron protruding from the red rocks upon which it had stood.

Henry Winstanley had been granted his wish. He had been in his lighthouse during "the greatest storm that ever was."

5

The builder of the next Eddystone light was also a singular man, but singular in a very different way from Henry Winstanley. The circumstances of his life made him singular, even mysterious; and his unsolved disappearance at what seems to have been its close only added to the mystery.

His name was John Rudyerd. He was the one decent member of a family of prodigious rascals. His father was an insignificant Cornish laborer. His brothers were so notorious for cruel behavior and even for crime that the family was feared well beyond the boundaries of its own village. It was described as "a worthless set of ragged beggars whom nobody would employ on account of the badness of their characters."

Apparently John, one of the younger sons, suffered constant abuse from a brutal father and bullying brothers. When he could stand his life no longer, he ran away to Plymouth. There he found work as a domestic servant with a now unknown but evidently kind man, who became so interested in the boy's ambition and courage that he sent him to school and, after he had spent some highly successful years as a student, started him off in business on his own. This John Rudyerd, at last freed from his renegade family, became a silk merchant in London.

Where he gained his knowledge of science and mechanics we do not know. Perhaps in a century so devoted to new discovery and experiment as was the seventeenth century in England, which had seen the founding of the Royal Society in 1640, he, in common with many other men of his day, made an avocation, a hobby, of such study. At all events, after Trinity House

in London, that corporation or guild founded under
Henry VIII to hold authority over the building of lighthouses, had transferrred the rights over the Eddystone
reef to a certain John Lovet of Plymouth, Rudyerd ap-
plied to Lovet for permission to erect a second lighthouse there. He was granted not only the permission but
also the practical knowledge and experience of two
master shipwrights from the English Navy to work with
him as his assistants.

The dead Henry Winstanley was, however, John
Rudyerd's best and most indispensable teacher. He
wisely determined to profit by Winstanley's serious
mistakes. First of all, he decided upon a far wider base
to be placed upon a platform of rock made much more
even in its surface. Instead of twelve rods of iron he re-
solved to sink thirty-six of them more deeply into his
more even surface, and, moreover, to dovetail them
together.

John Rudyerd decided also that wood was a far
safer material to withstand the force of waves than was
stone. Let the base of his tower be filled with rocks
within its iron uprights, he said, like the ballast carried
by wooden ships; but let wood, stout Devonshire oak,
alternate with carefully wrought blocks of granite to
build his tower. And, finally, let the entire tower be en-
cased in timber, which, like the hull of a good ship,

would resist the onslaughts of the sea.

Rudyerd thought of other innovations. All dec-orations, such as Winstanley had used, must be severely done away with. Such fripperies were only dangerous catchers of wind. His tower must be plain, circular in shape, and tapering always toward its top. There must be no flat surfaces to receive the gusts and the waves. And for additional strength he decided to add a central mast of strong timber, which, buried in the ballast at the base, should run up the tower to its summit after the manner of a strong spinal column.

John Rudyerd's tapering tower, seventy-one feet in height, was not so fancy as was Henry Winstanley's; but with all its stark plainness it was far more functional. He began it in July, 1706, with frettings and frustrations from winds and waves halting his work for days on end; heavy boatloads of granite and timber floating idly at Plymouth; sullen men cursing the skies and the sea. Two summers later, however, he was able to show a light within it, although it was not completed for yet another year.

This second Eddystone lighthouse threw its gleams for nearly fifty years. One long night, just before dawn in December of 1755, its lantern caught on fire. Those oaken timbers, in which its builder had placed such confidence, worm-eaten though some of them had become, proved tinder before a high wind; and its tower in a matter of minutes became a blazing torch. Its keepers escaped to the wet shelter of the rocks; but the lighthouse could not escape. It could but illumine the seas ominously and, indeed, splendidly, before it crashed in blazing bits into the turbulent waters.

No one has ever known what became of its builder. John Rudyerd has faded into the mists of history, vanished without a trace. Did he die, his death perhaps hastened by his cruel labor upon his tapering tower? Did he go to another country, perhaps to America, to try to forget his humiliation, his bitter disappointment, his sense of failure?

His end has never been discovered; but his experimental innovations in the building of lighthouse towers have remained to serve as his monument. He, too, was singular and remarkable; and the Eddystone has never forgotten him.

6

When one today sails toward Plymouth harbor and sees the great, gray, red-capped tower of the Eddystone light rising one hundred and thirty-six feet above the highest water line, he sees, too, not far from it a rather forlorn, yet sturdy piece of masonry, which is known as *Smeaton's Stump.* This, the haunt of countless seabirds, remains as the monument to the most remarkable of all the Eddystone builders. He was neither so unique as Henry Winstanley nor so mysterious as John Rudyerd; yet he was more memorable than either of his predecessors in his ideas both about lighthouses and about life.

Or was it his father who was remarkable? For John Smeaton in the harsh lottery of life drew a most unusual father for himself. The third Eddystone lighthouse owes its very being to John Smeaton's father. Without him there would have been no such lighthouse lasting well over one hundred years. Even today its brown stump with its clustering gulls and terns is a tribute to a tolerant, understanding, and wise man. Would there were more fathers like him in every land under the sun!

John Smeaton's father was a successful lawyer in Leeds, Yorkshire, a small country town when John was born in 1724, not the great commercial and industrial city which it is today. This father was a well-to-do, prosperous man, who lived in one of the grander houses just outside Leeds. He naturally wanted his only son to study law, to succeed him in his successful practice of it; and with this hope in his mind he sent John to a good school, where he was brilliant in mathematics, but rather dull at all other subjects. Nor was he at all interested in those sports and games in which English boys are assumed to participate with vast eagerness. He seemed, indeed, to his schoolfellows not only antisocial, but actually stupid; and they were not at all slow in ridiculing him.

There was one activity, however, in which young John Smeaton markedly excelled: work with his hands. He loved above all else to watch craftsmen at their jobs, carpenters, plumbers, bricklayers. He early learned to use tools of every kind; and nothing so fascinated him as invention and experiment. The deep desire of his father set him, after his school days, to reading law, which John hated. He lived only for the moment when he could escape from musty legal tomes and return to his own workshop, which his disappointed yet generous father had ordered made for him.

It must be remembered that in eighteenth-century England a boy who used tools, except as a mere hobby, was not considered a gentleman, but only an artisan. He was, in other words, stepping down from the professional class of men into that of a laborer. John's father, however, had the vision, the courage, and the wisdom to allow his only son to forsake the gentlemanly profession of the law in order that he might fulfill his own desires, humble as those desires might seem. Within a few years that son, who, instead of a barrister, became a mere apprentice to a maker of instruments, was so skilled at his work and so original in his thoughts that by the age of twenty-six he had not only set up his own business as an instrument maker, but he had also been invited by the exclusive Royal Society in London to read papers before its renowned scientists on compasses and other marine inventions.

John Smeaton, largely because of his father's tolerance and understanding, became the third builder of a lighthouse on the dreaded Eddystone reef. Nor was the lighthouse which he built there wrecked by monstrous winds or destroyed by flames. After one hundred and twenty-five years of incalculable help to mariners it became so out-of-date in the face of nineteenth-century technology that it gave place to a new one, as is the way of many good things in this world. The upper part of its tower was taken into Plymouth and set up there as a curiosity for visitors; its base remained, and still remains, upon the Eddystone rocks. John Smeaton's lighthouse was never truly vanquished. Nor was its builder.

John Smeaton, practical and realistic though he was,

was also an idealist, a visionary among men. He did not care for money or for fame. He cared only for the best job a man could do. All his life he loved work for the sake of work itself, its dignity, its possible perfection. He cared, too, and very deeply, for the contribution which a man's work might make to his fellowmen, to the world. For he devoutly believed that the ability of every man, whatever its nature, is but an obligation which he must discharge in behalf of the public welfare.

Smeaton arrived in Plymouth to begin his work in March of the year 1756 when he was thirty-two years old. He was happy and excited, for he was confident that his theories of design, over which he had spent days and nights of work and thought, were sound and practical. Nor did his excitement die even when for two long months the weather allowed him only ten trips to the reef. This subservience to the weather, nevertheless, made him determine against any town as a base for disgruntled, frustrated workmen; and one of his first decisions was to man and equip a stout boat which, anchored a quarter of a mile from the Eddystone, would be the floating home of his builders and which would also supply an inadequate, but helpful light, a sort of lightship for navigators. For this purpose a broad-beamed, tough herring boat, known as a *buss*, was fitted out. It was named the *Neptune Buss;* and although it rolled and tossed about in heavy seas, often broke from its moorings, and was constantly washed by waves and spray, it did make unnecessary long morning and evening journeys from and to the mainland.

John Smeaton's lighthouse took more than three years to build. It is impossible here to describe its various features; but a few of them are of great interest. Its base was far wider and heavier than those of the two which had preceded it; it was built entirely of granite, its great, circular stones being ridged, or dovetailed, so that every block fitted tightly not against, but *within* another; it constantly tapered in its height, like the trunk of a great tree, partly for reasons of weight, which Smeaton knew should be at its base, partly to withstand the waves which would curl around it rather than beat with their full force against it. The candles of its high lantern were first lighted on October 15, 1759.

During the years of its building not one fatality had occurred. No man had lost his life; no man had been severely injured. Every man had not only been generously paid for his work, but had been given extra wages for each hour spent upon the rock itself, where he was fated to be soaked and miserable. On the other hand, any man who failed in his duty was discharged at once.

Small wonder that Smeaton's workmen respected and admired him!

It was entirely characteristic of John Smeaton that he refused to have his name engraved upon his tower in the prominent position which had been suggested to him. Instead of his name, he chose two inscriptions to be cut in its stone. One was a verse from the 127th Psalm: *Except the Lord build the house, they labour in vain that build it.* The other, on the last stone to be set in place in late August, 1759, a stone just above the lantern door, was made of two words: *Laus Deo.*

John Smeaton's lighthouse was still gleaming when he died in 1792, and it was to send its light across the dangerous seas for nearly a century longer. He had surely paid whatever debt he owed to the public welfare in return for the gift of his life.

James Watt, that Scottish boy who watched his mother's teakettle and dreamed of a locomotive run by steam, thought and said that John Smeaton was a great man. He was.

7

The fourth and the final builder of a lighthouse on the Eddystone reef was named James Douglass. He, too, was a singular and a remarkable man. Within him were gathered all the most distinctive traits of his three predecessors. He had not a little of Henry Winstanley's oddity. The men who worked for him were puzzled by his love of playing a flute, and perhaps rather badly, although the sea birds seemed charmed by the precarious sounds which he drew from it. He had John Rudyerd's strong sense of the functional and a great deal of John Smeaton's idealism. He was, in a curious way, all three of them rolled into himself.

In one most important particular he was, however, different from them all. He was a man of the late nineteenth century; and he was equipped as they had not been with far more background and training than they had known. His father, Nicholas Douglass, had built lighthouses all his life; and James had been his willing and eager assistant. He and his brother William had, in fact, spent their childhood in the wild, remote places where their father had worked—on the Scilly Isles, where Nicholas Douglass had built the great Bishop Rock Light; in Wales where, off its desolate southwest tip, the Smalls Light had risen; at Land's End on the farthest bit of England, where on the dreaded Wolf Rock another high tower had reached skyward. The boys had gone to school as they could wherever they were, their best teacher always being their father himself. When at the age of thirty-six James Douglass was appointed by Trinity House in London as their chief engineer and was thereupon commissioned to erect a fourth lighthouse on the Eddystone, he brought to his work a boyhood and young manhood spent among lighthouses and a deep affection for them as well.

Like John Smeaton, whom James Douglass much admired, Douglass had a profound sense of the value of ordinary, average men and of their work. A deeply religious man himself, he always conducted a brief religious service each morning and each evening that work was done on the wave-swept rocks. His men called him "Captain Jim" and always spoke of him not only with deep respect, but with genuine affection. Some among them may have thought his religious practices curious and held under peculiar circumstances; but all admired his courage and his assurance that God also had an interest in the new Eddystone light.

James Douglass, of course, was fortunate in the possession of certain technical facilities available to him in 1878, innovations which his predecessors had never known. Winches and cranes could now lift and swing the massive blocks of granite into place upon his foundation. The cement of his day was more dependable than that which the earlier builders had used. Instead of hammers and pickaxes in the hands of workmen he had rock drills to pierce both the rocks of the Eddystone and his tons of granite. Nor was he so dependent upon the frustrating vagaries of wind and weather. A stout steamship, the *Hercules*, which brought those tons of stone out from Plymouth, could and did act as his floating workshop. It did not break its moorings and go adrift as John Smeaton's *Neptune Buss* had done.

Douglass planned his tower on the same central reef about forty yards from Smeaton's, a site which even at low tide was submerged. Nevertheless, he managed to construct a "coffer dam" of stone and concrete, which, pumped dry at each low tide during the daylight, formed his cylindrical base, forty-four feet in diameter, and which, being cylindrical, would break the greatest force of the waves and reduce their former tendency to dash up the tower to be erected upon it. To be sure, workmen were often up to the waist in water; yet they worked on, and with the help of the *Hercules* standing by with material and with hoisting machines, they could work many more days even in the early winter months.

From its lowest foundation rock the base of James Douglass's tower rose to a height of two and one-half feet above high water. The lighthouse tower itself rested upon a ledge, the wide summit of the foundation, and known to lighthouse men as the *setoff*. This setoff served as a landing stage for boats when the sea allowed them to approach, and for men swung across in slings over the raging waters when the boats which had brought them must toss about at some distance. The granite stones of both base and tower were more than dovetailed into one another. They were *locked* by great ridges of rock, ridges which were made possible by modern tools and which fitted closely into clefts cut in the stones above and alongside. Nineteenth-century England had made vast strides in mechanics and in engineering; and James Douglass had received from both many legacies entirely inaccessible to the builders who had gone before him.

The lantern of the fourth Eddystone tower, after four years of grueling labor, was lighted on May 19, 1882. Its light was supplied, not by candles, but by circular wicks fed by oil, and its beams were plainly visible across eighteen miles of sea.

James Douglass's tower of pale gray granite with a bright red crown still stands, proud, arrogant, and defiant, the conqueror of cruel waters. Five years ago, in 1959, its revolving lantern was replaced with an electrical lamp, of 1250-watt power, that power generated by three small engines in one of the lower tower rooms.

Its designer and builder, upon his completion of the fourth Eddystone lighthouse, was honored by a knighthood conferred upon him by Queen Victoria in grateful recognition of his masterly work not alone for England, but for all mankind. He was doubtless pleased and proud. Yet it was like him to cause to be engraved along the wall of the room just below the lantern the words which John Smeaton had placed in his lighthouse:

Except the Lord build the house, they labour in vain that build it.

IV

Deadly Foes of Lighthouses

LIGHTHOUSES SINCE THEIR BEGINNINGS HAVE known their enemies, their deadly foes, as cruel and as ruthless as are winds and waves. These foes have been human foes, grasping, wicked men who have wanted no lights to help ships and sailors, but who, instead, have longed and even prayed for ships to be cast on their own shores so that they might seize the cargoes, welcome drowned and broken bodies, enslave or murder any surviving sailors.

It is difficult to discover sober and accurate history

about these inhumane and bestial men, who have been known in our own language for nearly two hundred years as *wreckers*. They and their horrible deeds belong rather to the folklore of the sea than to its authentic history. Crimes and criminals are never easy to discover, to drag out from the darkness in which they lurk. And yet we know altogether too well that lonely, precipitous, dangerous coastlines throughout the world have nurtured such men who have lived and prospered by means of death and disaster. Tradition, bolstered always by the sad reality of human nature at its worst, insists that there were such monstrous men even on Greek and Roman shores and that the slavery of ancient days was increased by many a sailor who had escaped death by shipwreck only to face a living death by pulling a heavy oar in a galley for the rest of his life.

The history and traditions of our own country are in no sense free from these dark blots. The rocky shores of New England apparently knew early of the existence and the horrible activity of wreckers. Parts of the Massachusetts coastline, particularly in the neighborhoods of Cape Cod and Cape Ann, were smirched and disgraced by such crime in the eighteenth and early nineteenth centuries. The sandy shoals of the first and the sharp rocks of the second were veritable deathtraps for ships in the years before our shores became well lighted. And their lighthouses were hated, despised, and feared by men who not only watched and waited for ships to founder or to crash, but who actually devised cruel means to bring about such tragedy.

2

Yet although America bears her own share of such heinous conduct, parts of England and Scotland seem, alas! to deserve more guilt or at least to preserve more hair-raising tales of it than do any other regions toward which many ships sail. This deplorable fact is the result, of course, of the nature of their shores. Scotland, east, north, and west, is a rockbound land; and one or two centuries ago its coasts were lonely and uninhabited enough for wreckers to ply their dangerous and evil pursuits with relatively little fear of detection. Dwellers on the Shetland and Orkney Islands, on the high eastern headlands west of where the great Bell Rock Light now stands, and on the jagged, perilous shores of the Hebrides, or Western Islands, might be sure, if they were by nature inhumane men or if they were unable to resist temptation and corruption, that the angry seas would all too frequently send a ship crashing on their rocks and reefs. The rocky, dangerous Scilly Isles in the English Channel afforded also constant assurance of spoils for wreckers. Far too many inhabitants of the Scillies deplored the building of the Bishop Rock Light in 1858! The very fact, which history does record, that over a space of twenty-three years, between 1823 and 1846, one hundred and thirty-one vessels were lost on a single forty-mile strip of the coast of Cornwall proves beyond doubt that wicked men might be sure of ample material upon which to exercise most profitably their evil genius.

Cornwall, indeed, bears the dark distinction of being the most renowned home of wreckers. Its very isolation in the extreme west of England, the ragged, merciless character of its high coastline, especially in the north, the poverty of many of its people, notably its miners, or *tinners* as they were locally known, gave it early a sinister reputation for the pillage and the plunder of ships. And not only the poor were involved in such wicked enterprise. Certain of its so-called "gentry" and even vicars of churches were numbered among its scoundrels. It is said, indeed, that parsons of far outlying seaside parishes were urged by some of their parishioners not, of course, to pray for wrecks, but to urge God, if, in His providence, wrecks *must* happen, to guide them in the right direction!

Many of the hideous tales of wreckers can surely be abandoned to the folklore to which they belong. Many more should not be allowed to dim the daring and noble attempts made by countless Cornishmen to lend assistance to the crews of ships cast upon their rocks and reefs. And yet, that wreckers did follow their ghoulish and terrifying trade in many a remote Cornish seaside settlement has never been denied, even by the most sober and dependable of historians. Details may be impossible to discover; but the fact that such details existed is without question.

Wreckers were far too certain of rare and luxurious treasures to listen to the still, small voice of their better natures. Foundered or broken ships meant food, choice wines and liquors, silks, precious woods, silver and gold, often actual money in the coinage of many lands. Such ships with their cargoes were looked upon by bad men as godsends, and the looting of them as an adventure, dangerous and costly, to be sure, yet highly valuable to homes, to kitchen larders, and to greedy, unprincipled men and women.

3

The most horrible aspect of wrecking was its encouragement, the various devices by means of which it might be assured. These devices, the fruit of shrewd, unscrupulous minds, were several. The display of false lights was perhaps the most commonly employed. Such lights, carefully placed on a dangerous headland or above a treacherous reef, lured many a confused navigator to his doom. Assuming them to be the signs of life and habitation, he drove his ship toward them only to be met by swift destruction and disaster.

Especially original and diabolical minds conceived the further perfidious idea of making these lights resemble those of a ship in motion. To attach two or three lanterns to the broad back of a Cornish pony and then to lead him along a cliff path or just above a particularly hazardous cove supplied most realistically to a ship's pilot the belief that another vessel was making toward a safe anchorage and might well be followed shoreward.

Wreckers were familiarly known as *moon-cussers*, since they, of course, needed darkness above all else for the pursuit of their nefarious doings. Storm and fog were their friends and their allies. Murder became quite logically included among their activities since dead men tell no tales. It was easy to hold a struggling man or a woman from some passenger ship beneath the water until there should be no danger either from escape or from unwanted, perhaps perilous talk.

The glow from a lighthouse tower was, of course, their bitter and most dreaded enemy. From the beginning of the building of such safeguards to sailors they began to fear for the future of their shameful avocation. When the lighthouse at the Lizard Point in Cornwall was decided upon, no subject was so unpopular among the remote villages of the Cornish coasts. Women began to fear that they might no longer go about in rich apparel; men began to be anxious about strange, yet *gold* coins jingling in their pockets and about bottles of the best wine from faraway vineyards. The only lights which wreckers valued were those false ones by which they decoyed, hoodwinked, and murdered their innocent victims.

4

Every reader of this story of lighthouses should read also and as soon as possible a thrilling and wonderful novel about these foes of light, the wreckers of one or more centuries ago. It is called *Jamaica Inn*, and it was written by an English author, Daphne du Maurier. I know of no other account which so clearly and so horribly describes these loathsome men and their outrageous deeds.

Jamaica Inn still stands on Bodmin Moor in Cornwall. It looks quiet and respectable enough now and is
both, in spite of its lonely location; but in Miss du Maurier's story it was once the repository for the spoil of
wreckers, and its terrifying landlord was their leader.
He was a gigantic man, this Joshua Merlyn, and he
feared nothing but his own drunken orgies, over which
he had no control and which might keep him from his
dreadful pastime. To him the murder of men was of far
less consequence than a call from the local squire, an
honest man who was rightly suspicious of Jamaica Inn,
its landlord, and its devilish frequenters.

The heroine of this fascinating tale is a Cornish
girl named Mary Yellan. Her suffering at the hands of
evil men and her incredible courage finally bring to
light, and to the law, the horrible outrages perpetrated
at night upon the shore of a dangerous and lonely cove.
She thinks, as do we all until the very end of the story,
that the landlord of Jamaica Inn, who is her uncle, is
the leading spirit of this gang of desperadoes. But he
isn't. He may well be the most ruthless and wicked man
among them; yet there is another more daring and
wicked than he—another who is the archcriminal of
them all.

Hurry to the nearest library or bookshop to discover

who this outcast from all decent people really is. And *don't* begin this dramatic and completely absorbing book by turning first to its close, a common failing of unintelligent readers. From its first chapter, its first page about the stagecoach climbing the hill in the rainy night, you will be enthralled; and you will never forget these deadly foes of lighthouses—foes now no more because of stringent laws against them and because of the spread of population to the remoter corners of the earth.

They once lived, however, by violence and murder; and they are a very real part of the story of lighthouses. For their dearest desire was that no light-bearing tower should ever rise from reef, island, or headland to help a sailor or to save a ship.

✤ V ✤

The Loneliest and
Most Dangerous of Our
Own Rocks and Reefs

To PLAN AND TO ERECT A LIGHTHOUSE ON A SIZA-
ble island, remote though it may be, or on a beetling
headland, dangerous though it is, has always been a
relatively easy accomplishment. In both places there is
land—land upon which safe and dry workmen can labor
through all daylight hours; land for the homes of keepers, for sheds built to contain fog signals, engineer's
materials, necessary engines themselves; land in these
latter days for the generation of electricity; sometimes
enough land for gardens and for trees, even for a

solitary cow or two. There is land for the drawing up of small boats and for a slip to receive courageous visitors.

Reefs such as the Eddystone have no land about them. Instead they jut precipitously from the open sea to tax all the ingenuity and courage which the hardiest of men possess. All the world knows the Eddystone; all the world honors its builders as the first who dared to attempt the mastery of a lonely, sea-swept rock; all the world honors, too, the least and the most humble of its English workmen. Yet the proud daughter of England, the United States of America, has won her triumphs, too, upon her own rocks and reefs, triumphs later, to be sure, but comparable to the Bishop Rock Light, the Bell on the Inchcape Rock, even to the Eddystone itself. Why not, then, for this chapter, stay within the watery boundaries of our own country and take pride in the work of our own lighthouse builders on the most inhospitable of our own rocks and reefs?

Sometimes our reefs are sunken and hence more ugly; sometimes, instead, they are small, barren islets composed entirely of jagged rocks. Off the United States there are four particularly renowned lights, constructed upon the most desolate of reefs or upon these islets of rock. Nor are they all that we have of such wonders;

but since they are the best-known and most famous, shall we not look at them one by one in order to discover the problems which they presented to our builders, the havoc which their lonely and dangerous sites had caused before and even after their lighthouses arose, and the pride which we should justly feel in our possession of them?

Two of our most lonely and dangerous rocks and reefs lie off the deeply indented coast of Maine, which, with all its bays, promontories, inlets, and estuaries, is twenty-five hundred miles in length, a distance nearly as great as that across our country from the Atlantic to the Pacific. These two are the rocky islets of Mount Desert and Matinicus. A third is off the Massachusetts shoreline, Minot's Ledge on the Cohasset reefs. The fourth is a Pacific rock, rising from the sea one mile off the coast of Oregon. It is called Tillamook.

Each of the lighthouses which stand on these rocky islets or these reefs is a monument to the minds and to the hands of brave men. Let us picture each in its isolation and in so doing honor the courage of their makers, whether of their engineers or of the unknown yet stalwart men who swung their pickaxes and escaped or did *not* escape the waves and the spray dashing over them.

89

2

Mount Desert Rock, which should not be confounded with the island of the same name, is without doubt the loneliest of all United States light stations. Matinicus is lonely, too, but it does have islands about. Matinicus Island, with its considerable settlement, is only six miles away. Boon Island Light, near York, Maine, is lonely, also; yet it is only nine miles from the mainland. Mount Desert Rock is over twenty miles from any land at all, rock, ledge, island, or piece of mainland.

Mount Desert Rock does not rise, to be sure, as a group of angry pinnacles out of a boiling ocean. It is, instead, a half-acre of rock, large enough even for a small group of buildings, houses for its keeper and his assistants, shelters for its necessary supplies and machines. The loneliness, which has long been its distinction since Champlain sailed cautiously by it in the year 1604, lies in its isolated situation, in the grassless, treeless character of its bleak granite surface, in the terrible raging onslaught of the waves across it. Even when the sea is smooth, which is seldom enough around Mount Desert Rock, the highest point of its tiny island is only some seventeen feet above high water; and in winter storms the entire rock is mercilessly swept by gigantic waves. It is impossible to realize the force of such waves even when we know that they have been capable of moving a boulder weighing seventy-five tons out of its place on this barren shelf of rock.

Women and children no longer live on Mount Desert Rock. They once did, however, quite as a matter of course, if their husbands and fathers were keepers of the light there. And because they lived there, they have endowed Mount Desert Rock with a story as unusual and fascinating in its way as is any story of shipwreck and disaster. It is true that a woman there once fed and cared for nine men whose boat had crashed against the rocks, saving them all from serious illness, perhaps from death. It is equally true that a succession of women and children, through hope and faith and hard work, gave to their bleak and lonely home a name and a reputation unique among remote and distant islands of rock.

For many years the women and children of Mount Desert Rock followed a lovely custom, which the coast of Maine and those who have cruised its waters will long remember. With touching trust that the brief summer months might free them from the monstrous storms of winter, they used to wedge handfuls of soil into the highest crevices of their rocky home and plant seeds

91

there. Kindly fishermen on their way past the Rock used to bring them a bag or two of well-fertilized earth, which they would cram into slits and holes and hollows and then plant seeds in their carefully hoarded soil—flower and vegetable seeds, seeds of nasturtiums, zinnias, bachelor's-buttons, seeds of carrots, lettuce, peas, and beans, which might afford a welcome change to their monotonous meals. Mount Desert Rock has always had plenty of light and sunshine during the summer; and, with good luck and hard work, it became each summer a garden of color rising out of the gray sea. Rubies, sapphires, topazes, and always emeralds glowed and sparkled there, when there were women and children on the Rock and when the weather in late spring and during the summer was mercifully kind.

God's Rock Garden was the name given to this isolated Mount Desert Rock during those brief summer months; and, although His garden by November was sure to be swept as bare as the rocks themselves, it has, nevertheless, remained a bright memory to many Maine coast mariners.

Mount Desert Rock has had its light since 1830, and a better, farther-sweeping one since it was improved in 1857 and again in 1898. Its tower is not a tall one; too frequent and too thick fog makes mere height unwise;

but it is a sturdy lighthouse, built with a broad base and thick walls. It is sixty feet high above its menacing rock.

Today men of the Coast Guard look upon it as the loneliest of stations; and before their day its usual four keepers in charge were likely to welcome a change. It has known shipwrecks in plenty during its long life, ships dashed upon its own ledges through merciless winds and tides. Yet for years around the turn of the present century and for a score of years thereafter it had its garden, too, made by the toil and the eagerness of its women and its lonely children. Even today there are those who remember the glow of its flowers as well as the glow of its light.

A few years ago in a Massachusetts city I met a woman who had been a little girl on Mount Desert Rock.

"Wasn't it a frightfully lonely life away out there?" I asked her.

"I don't think it was," she said. "I lived there when I was nine years old until I was well past thirteen. I often think it gave me the best things I've ever known. The gulls used to eat out of my hand. And one summer I counted twenty nasturtiums in my own garden that I had made from cramming handfuls of soil into the holes in the rock. I can raise all the flowers I like now without a wind or a wave to worry about. But they're not like those twenty nasturtiums springing out of that cruel rock.

"The people who sailed past called it God's Rock Garden, but it was really *mine*. I never gave Him my garden; but I've thanked Him all my life for Mount Desert Rock."

3

Matinicus Rock is also a barren island, and its light-house a desolate and lonely tower. It is not a mere islet like Mount Desert Rock; it contains, in fact, some thirty acres of sharp ledges rising from the sea at the entrance to Penobscot Bay. Yet no grass is bold enough to sprout there, no tough, windswept shrub or weed. Matinicus with all its rough, sharp acres is swept as bare as is Mount Desert Rock by winds and waves to which mere acreage is as nothing. Its rocks rise in one place to a sharp, high ridge; but even this height has small power to halt or to stem overwhelming seas.

There has been a light on Matinicus Rock since 1827. In fact, for just short of one hundred years there were two towers there, each securely connected with the other, north and south, by a row of buildings, houses for the keeper and his assistants, other buildings for necessary equipment. These twin towers, at first made of wood, were replaced in 1857 by stouter ones of granite. In 1923 the northern tower was discontinued.

Matinicus Rock has always been famous for its storms, or, in Maine words, its "gales of wind." Penobscot Bay, especially at its wide entrance, is most familiar with "dirty weather." Even as late as November, 1950, while a crew of Coast Guardsmen was in charge of the light, a most violent storm so battered the Rock that its waves not only swept over the entire island, but actually smashed the glass of the lantern and extinguished the light itself, after making rubble of the strong sea wall and a twisted mass of the engines, generators, and radio equipment.

November is perhaps the most dire and hateful word in the language to those few intrepid souls who have charge of the lighthouse on Matinicus Rock. December, January, and February will most likely present their fearsome offerings, too; but as months to be watched and dreaded, they pale before November. November is the archfiend, who in his lowering, dismal thirty days is certain to be harboring with his own horrid mockery a northeast gale.

Nevertheless, it was January in the year 1857 which gave to Matinicus Rock its most awful storm on record and endowed a fourteen-year-old girl with fame still enduring in the annals of lighthouse history. This girl's name was Abbie Burgess. Her father, Samuel Burgess, was at that time keeper of Matinicus Rock light, with his young son as his only helper; for not until four years later did the Lighthouse Service realize that more men were necessary on a station so remote and dangerous as Matinicus Rock.

Captain Burgess, one of the most reliable and experienced of keepers, had gone in his sailboat on the morning preceding the coming of the storm, to Matinicus Island, six miles away for necessary provisions. Food was becoming dangerously scarce on the Rock. He had meant to be away a few daylight hours at most. Instead, he and his son, who, frightened over the suddenly threatening weather, had gone by dory to join his father and to help him with the supplies, were unable because of the monstrous seas to return to the Rock for three weeks.

During those three weeks, while winds reached hurricane force, bringing sleet, snow, and gigantic sweeping seas, Abbie Burgess, unaided, tended the two lights. She lent hope to her mother, who was ill from anxiety and fear, cared for two younger sisters, watched the family's small store of food steadily diminish; yet in the face of toil, fright, hunger, and the constant threat of death, she saw to it that the lights did not fail. Climbing stairs all night long, making her way from the tower at the north to that at the south, trimming wicks and carrying oil, she labored on for twenty-one days and nights as the sole keeper of the lights on Matinicus Rock.

It is Abbie Burgess, who, after more than a century, is remembered whenever Matinicus Rock is named or whenever its rugged outlines are seen by those who sail past it. Its desolation and danger have long bestowed fame and fear upon it. Abbie Burgess at the age of fourteen gave it immortality.

4

The most ruthless and cruel of our rocks and reefs lies off the coast of Massachusetts, near Cohasset, and only some six miles from the entrance to Boston harbor. It might well be called our American Eddystone because of its treachery and its ugliness. It is Minot's Ledge; and it gets its name in ironic memory of its destruction in the year 1754 of a valuable ship belonging to a Boston merchant called George Minot.

Minot's Ledge, the most dangerous of many submerged rocks about Cohasset, has been rightly termed the *killer* among all our most perilous reefs. A year before its first lighthouse was built in 1850 after two years of back-breaking labor, the Cohasset reefs claimed the lives of a veritable shipload of Irish immigrants, men, women, and children. In the thirty years between 1817 and 1847 shipwrecks around Minot's cost half a hundred human lives and an equal number of ships. In a brief nine years from 1833 to 1842 forty vessels were pounded to bits, and on six of these every man of their crews perished.

Perhaps the most awful tragedy took place only a little more than a year after the completion of its first tower and the showing of its first light on New Year's Day, in 1850. During a monstrous gale in April, 1851, the lighthouse itself crashed into the sea, taking with it the two keepers in its tower. Widespread public sorrow and indignation over this tragic disaster resulted in the determination on the part of our Lighthouse Service to raise a second lighthouse sturdy enough to withstand any storm which the Atlantic Ocean might produce in its most wicked mood; and in 1855 under the supervision of a highly qualified captain in the United States Engineering Corps, a man named Barton Alexander, the work was begun. Later on, during our Civil War, this same man was to show the same genius, both in handling men and in dealing with the projects of army engineering.

The seemingly insuperable conquest of a reef, only three and a half feet above the lowest tide, was comparable in many ways with that of the Eddystone; and many of Captain Alexander's plans, improved and furthered, of course, by much progress in science and technology, were similar to the Eddystone pioneers'. He, too, drove iron shafts into the rock; he, too, dovetailed his great granite blocks and, as James Douglass was to do thirty years later at the Eddystone, locked them to one another by deep ridges; he, too, provided a nearby boat both for a home and a floating workshop; and he, too, like Henry Winstanley, John Rudyerd, and John Smeaton, was not above working with his men, and like them, being drenched to the skin and in constant danger.

Massachusetts Bay knew perhaps its worst winter on record in 1856–57, with such bitter cold that Boston Harbor was frozen, with thousands of people walking and even driving their horses excitedly on its thick ice. Much of Captain Alexander's initial work because of cold and the accumulation of ice had to be done over again, so that it was not until the summer of 1857 that the first stone of his tower was actually laid. More than three years later, in November, 1860, Minot's Ledge lantern flashed its beacon, which was to continue to flash throughout a century even until now.

Perhaps the reception of the great light was as thrilling as was its lighting. For as its beams streamed out over the darkening November seas and illuminated even the shores, scores of bonfires, piled in readiness for their own lighting, sent their welcoming, triumphant flames toward the skies. Roman candles and sky-rockets burst forth into countless stars of praise along the Cohasset shoreline and from the docks of Boston. Church bells pealed, and men and women who had known tragedy and sorrow from those long unguarded reefs were not ashamed of the tears which ran down their faces.

Minot's Ledge is not only the most dangerous of our rocks and reefs, but its solitary lighthouse tower, one hundred and fourteen feet in height from its hidden base, ranks among the chief of the great sea-rock lighthouses throughout the world because of the skill and science employed in its construction. It shares these honors with Bishop Rock, with Bell Rock, and even with the Eddystone itself. So lonely is it as a sea-swept dwelling place that in the days of its keepers under the United States Lighthouse Service their families lived in houses built on shore, only the men themselves being

100

allowed in its tower.

Some of the highest waves conceivable have crashed and still crash against the gray, circular sides of Minot's tapering tower. Some are said to outdistance one hundred and fifty feet in height; many curl and soar well over the lantern itself. Yet still it stands, rising, with no ledge in sight, straight up from the boiling cauldron of the cold, relentless seas.

Now its lantern needs no men to light it. For nearly twenty years no keepers have felt loneliness and terror in the worst of winter storms. An automatic electric signal has taken the place of their anxious minds and careful hands. Every thirty seconds it repeats the number 143, in a series of brilliant flashes which punctuate the darkness, the fog, and the storms: one flash, four flashes, three flashes with a brief interval between each.

Not a few imaginative, romantic souls have translated this 143, these three figures, into three words. They claim that the flashes from Minot's Ledge now say "I-love-you" throughout the hours of the night. Such an idea seems at variance, to say the least, with its dark past, with the tragedies and the sufferings it has caused to ships and men.

Perhaps, these translators of its signal say, it is repentant, now that it has been conquered, and is humbly eager to make amends for its sins. Perhaps it is. Who knows?

5

We must leave Atlantic seas for those of the Pacific to look upon the fourth of our most desolate and dangerous rocks. In general, Pacific shores are less perilous, high in many places, to be sure, but less indented, less needful of lighthouses than are the rugged coasts of the Atlantic. Still, there is one spectacular and cruel Pacific rock, which rises in utter loneliness off the coast of Oregon, nineteen miles south of the mouth of the Columbia River and one mile west of the remote, reef-strewn coastline itself.

The wickedness of this rock, like its name, stretches far back into Indian days, long before our Great West was opened. One can be sure that any venturesome Chinook canoes gave it a wide berth! Its sheer, forbidding sides rise seventy-one feet above high water, which in places is more than one hundred feet in depth. And nowhere are Pacific waters more menacing and evil.

Tillamook Rock was responsible, indeed, for so many disasters to ships sailing up and down the western coast in those prosperous days after the discovery of gold in California, or setting forth from Washington and Oregon ports for new trade with Hawaii, that in the decades following the Civil War demands for a lighthouse on its jagged, ugly summit became so many and so clamorous that Congress was forced to pay heed to them. Even so, it was slow in providing adequate sums for the enormous cost of a tower there, cost which entailed among other huge expenditures the building of a twenty-mile-long mountain road for the carrying of supplies from the nearest town of any importance. It was not until the year 1879 that the rough top of Tillamook Rock began to be leveled by the cautious use of dynamite.

Tillamook generously offered more handicaps and hardships to its engineer and its workmen than perhaps any other sea-swept rock has ever presented. Not so well-known as Minot's Ledge because of its location off a less familiar coast, it yet rivaled Minot's in hazards and dangers. After its summit had been leveled at great cost and greater peril, the problems of the lighthouse itself had to be met and solved. The chief among these was the difficulty of getting men on and off the Rock, the steep sides of which offered little foothold even when the sea allowed the approach of a boat.

103

Small craft soon proved themselves worthless in the angry waters around Tillamook. They were as unreliable as so many chips. The depth and turbulence of the seas allowed no mere schooner to lie nearby and to serve both as a home and a workshop. The supply ship for Tillamook Rock had to be a sizable steam tender, large and heavy enough to house cranes and derricks as well as men. And finally, after long weeks of sorry and even fateful experimenting, the simplest, easiest, and safest way for workmen to reach their drenched and dangerous goal was found to be by a sort of crude chair, which moved by cable from the steam tender to the Rock and which carried its venturesome human burdens, one by one, above the tossing waves to deposit them upon the summit.

Upon this summit, the pinnacles and spurs of which had been blasted away by charges of dynamite, the one-story stone dwelling was built for the keepers of the light, together with a small house for fog sirens. From almost the exact center of the keepers' house the granite light-tower arose, sixty-two feet from base to lantern. Though the height of Tillamook had been diminished in order to make a safe foundation for its lighthouse, it in itself contributed so generously to the height of its tower that together they rose one hundred and thirty-three feet above the sea.

After less than two years of stupendous labor Tillamook Rock was lighted in February, 1881. It was four weeks too late, alas! to save the lives of twenty men, when in a thick fog an English ship crashed ashore only a mile above Tillamook, a tragic disaster which saddened all the weary men as they were setting the final stones to their tower and placing the sheets of heavy glass in the framework of their lantern.

Tillamook Light has thus far defied all dire predictions of its own certain disaster. It was known as the *hoodoo light,* and in many minds destined for swift and awful destruction from winds and raging seas. Gloomy prophets declared that no keepers could be found willing to live in its lighthouse, no men mad enough to risk their lives in tending its lantern. Yet they have been found, five of them at all times because of the extreme loneliness and danger of their Rock. And Tillamook Light still has not failed throughout nearly a hundred years.

A man named Charles Ballantyne was the engineer who was bold enough to attack and to vanquish Tillamook. His years of toil for his country are long since forgotten; even his name is now remembered by only a few; yet his courage and his skill should not be allowed to die. For he is among that gallant company of early American lighthouse engineers, men who, with more initiative and invention than formal training, risked their lives for other men, strangers yet friends since they, too, were conquerors of the seas as they sailed their ships.

Tillamook Rock and its lighthouse, which together rise so sharply from the Pacific, form Charles Ballantyne's most lofty monument. He could not have a more impressive one.

✤ VI ✤

The Lighting of Lighthouse Lanterns

THE LANTERNS OF ALL LIGHTHOUSES GIVE THEM their light and their meaning. Without lanterns their tapering towers, erected no matter at what cost to the lives of builders, would be as nothing. Every granite stone is hoisted and mortared into place for one purpose only: to hold a lamp which shall promise light and life to men who sail the seas.

Through the long centuries from the Pharos of Alexandria to Minot's Ledge and Tillamook Rock these lamps have been perfected from their early burning of wood and later of coal to the automatic flashing of powerful electric bulbs. Let us now trace in as clear and simple a way as possible the interesting story of that perfecting and that progress.*

2

The earliest lighthouses in all parts of the world without any doubt used wood fires to light their lanterns; and this most accessible of fuel continued to be used even by important towers in Europe well into the eighteenth century. Often the wood burned in the open air; sometimes it was covered by a metal roof to shield it from rain or snow. The difficulties presented by burning wood are easily imagined: the frequent carrying of the wood to the summit of towers; the constant attendance which it demanded; the smoke and soot which it inevitably produced; the lack of steadiness and of strength inherent in its flames. Once coal began to be mined widely in Europe, especially in England, coal

* This chapter is in no sense a scientific one; nor is it treated exhaustively. To boys and girls who know something of physics or who are primarily interested in science I would recommend the reading of those excellent articles on lighthouses and their lighting in the encyclopedias *Britannica* and *Americana*. I would also urge the study of the final chapter of *The World's Lighthouses before 1820,* by D. Alan Stevenson, Oxford University Press, 1959. This chapter gives a fine treatment of early means of lighting and of experiments with reflectors and with lenses.

fires, of course, alternated with those of wood for lantern use; but although these fires burned longer and required less attention than those of wood, they also gave forth smoke and soot, and they also meant the labor of transportation.

The humble household candle worsted them both. In the Middle Ages as soon as panes of glass for lanterns became both clearer and heavier and could be made without great expense, tallow candles began to be widely used as lighthouse illuminants. These candles, of course, were of large size, some weighing as much as two pounds; and they were often placed in circles within the lantern space. Although their wicks had to be trimmed frequently to avoid guttering, these tallow candles gave a comparatively steady flame and surely afforded the cleanest form of light before the common use of oil lamps in the late eighteenth century. Even the first two Eddystone towers, those of Winstanley and Rudyerd, were lighted by candles, some twenty-four in number and arranged in circular tiers within the lantern enclosure.

The oil lamp revolutionized the lighting of lighthouse lanterns, especially as it was perfected in the year 1782. Lamps burning oil had been used, however, long before that important date. One is recorded in Genoa, Italy, in the famous Lanterna lighthouse as early as 1449, when an uncle of Christopher Columbus was its keeper. And yet the early oil-burning lamps also gave out smoke and soot which darkened the panes of the lantern and thus dimmed its light.

A young Swiss scientist named Ami Argand, when he was in his twenties, discovered in 1782 a cure for this trouble by his invention of a circular wick to burn within a circular glass chimney, which by its enclosure of the wick lent both steadiness and safety to the flame, and hence greater cleanliness. Shortly afterward he invented a reflector, which would tend to throw the gleam of his light much farther into the distance beyond the lantern panes. This young man will always bear the distinction of contributing more toward the illumination of lighthouse lanterns than any other man has ever done; and, although in his lifetime he failed to find either protection or patronage for his wonderful invention and died in poverty in Geneva in 1803, his Argand lamp will never be forgotten.

His very discovery of it is a fascinating tale for us all and especially for boys who love experiment and invention on their own. He and his brother were playing around one evening at their work-table with small sticks of lighted wood. When the flame of one of these burned a bit too fiercely, Ami seized the neck of a broken bottle, which quite by happy chance was lying on the table, and covered the rampant flame with the cylinder of glass. Immediately he saw how the flame was controlled and steadied. In that exciting moment the Argand lamp was born; and in that exciting moment, too, while the brothers clapped each other on the back in their pride and joy, the long, fumbling story of the lanterns of lighthouses took a sharp turn for the better, although those two brothers could not then foresee the future which their experimenting had assured.

Had Ami Argand lived only until the year 1819, when the number of listed lighthouses, standing near or within the seas of the world, was given as two hundred and fifty-four, he might have learned that of this number two hundred and seventeen were already lighted by oil lamps patterned on his own. He would have learned also that the overwhelming majority of that latter number were using reflectors, also based on his own invention, to throw their lights farther abroad.

3

Until well into the twentieth century oil lamps patterned after those of Argand were the most widespread and the most efficient means of lighthouse illumination. In our own country they have been used for over a century and a half; and there is a strong probability, though no entirely authentic record, that even our first lighthouse, that off Boston in 1716, was lighted by some kind of oil lamp. Certainly all United States lights since around 1812 have at some time in their history been illumined by oil; and there are still those which continue to use it, if they are too far away from dependable electric outlets or too isolated or sea-bound for space for their own generators. Gas has been used also, either natural gas for lights located near its supply, or compressed gas in tanks; yet it has never been a real rival of oil.

I remember well how, in many light towers off the coast of Maine in the years around 1920, I watched the keepers trim their circular wicks and then draw their oil-filled lanterns upward so that with the first fall of darkness they might begin to revolve slowly downward on the grooved steel shaft on which they moved. Every four hours all night one keeper after another on watch would mount the many stairs of his winding staircase to raise his lantern to the top of its shaft in preparation for its slow, revolving descent.

Argand's circular wick lamp was improved in the

nineteenth century by the mantle lamp, known familiarly as the Aladdin lamp, which gave a much more powerful light with a smaller consumption of kerosene. This
type of oil lamp has been used in many important lanterns, like that of Cape Hatteras, and sometimes with
a cluster of mantles to ensure yet greater brilliancy.

Various kinds of oil have been tried over the years,
sperm, fish, coconut, colza, lard. Kerosene, however, or
paraffin oil, as it is called in England, has been found
to be the best and the least expensive of them all. And
plain, old-fashioned, household kerosene, like the humble candle, has been slow in surrendering its dominance
of lighthouse lanterns throughout the world.

4

Electricity was used in England for lighthouse
illumination some seventy-five years before it was used
in our country; but it was abandoned in favor of good
old kerosene, or paraffin, on at least one important light
station since it was found to be too costly. In the United
States electricity's first use seems to have been the lighting of the Statue of Liberty in 1886. After that signal
event, lighthouses in the area of New York harbor began
to install electric bulbs in their lanterns.

For the lighting of the lanterns of remote or dangerous lighthouse towers, where the lives of keepers are necessarily lonely and hazardous, the electric bulb has proved an unquestionable boon. As we have seen, Minot's Ledge now has no keepers. Electricity has made it an automatic light. The Eddystone still has its keepers; but now that engines affording electrical power are stored in its great tower, their task is far less onerous and demanding than it was in the days of oil.

Many lighthouses along our dangerous Atlantic coast are now lighted by electric bulbs, from the lofty light of Cape Hatteras to those at the summits of far lesser shafts. Many towers which once knew their keepers know them no longer; and their homes have gone with their occupants. Thus "the old order changeth, yielding place to new" in Tennyson's words; and yet the old order fostered a courage and an adventure which the new will never know.

5

The light in a lighthouse lantern must not only be kindled. It must as well be thrown far and wide across the sea. And for this purpose a lens is necessary.

As did Ami Argand in the late eighteenth century,

so did a French physicist, named Augustin Fresnel, in the early nineteenth change, again *revolutionize,* the story of lighthouses. It was he who developed the use of the lens, surrounded by rings of glass prisms, which could throw the beams of light to a great distance.

Fresnel was more fortunate than was young Ami Argand. His invention was seized upon at once by those institutions and boards which govern the lighthouses of all countries. In the United States by the time of the outbreak of our Civil War, lenses had been installed in practically all our lighthouse lanterns; and this install-ment has been generally true throughout the world.

6

The time may well come—indeed, prophets claim it is not far off, but near—when the very idea of a keeper tending his light will seem as much of an absurdity as it is an anachronism; when shore-based, radio beacons will make even lighthouses themselves completely out of date and unnecessary.

Yet when that time comes, when perfected ma-chinery has taken the place of lamps, of fog blasts and sirens, even of brave men, let us hope that our right-ful pride may not be without its regret. May there still be those, both young and old, who will be sad over the passing away of tall granite towers, built by valor and self-sacrifice on reefs and headlands, sad even that tallow candles and oil lamps have had their day, sad that the spirit and the hands of man are no longer called upon to triumph as they once triumphed in the face of danger and death for the sake of human life and the safety of ships.

✤ VII ✤

The Life of Boys and Girls on Lighthouse Stations

I HAVE BEEN EXTREMELY FORTUNATE IN KNOWING personally, even intimately, many boys and girls who in the years between 1918 and 1935 were living on light stations. I was young myself during those years of our friendship; and they were far younger. I know some of them as men and women even today; and they always talk of those lighthouse years as the best years of their lives just as did the woman who had proudly raised her twenty nasturtiums on Mount Desert Rock.

At that time the fathers of these boys and girls were

121

the keepers of the lights; and during the summer months of those years I knew well both the keepers and their families through my association with the Maine Seacoast Mission, which has always had as an important part of its work the visiting of the many Maine coast lighthouses. This Mission, founded some seventy-five years ago, has since its beginning worked among outlying seacoast settlements, bringing on its boat, the *Sunbeam* (which the Maine coast calls *God's tug-boat*), books, cheer, quite undenominational religious services, medicines, Christmas gifts, a doctor when one is desperately needed, and a glimpse of the outside world to lonely remote islands and more lonely lighthouses.

I sailed on the *Sunbeam* for many summers, giving whatever small service I could to the founder of the Mission, Dr. Alexander MacDonald, a Scotsman trained at Bowdoin College both in the liberal arts and in medicine. He was truly a wonderful man, humorous, humane, adaptable to literally any circumstance, vigorous, tireless, and a friend to hundreds of Maine islanders, fishermen, lighthouse keepers, and their families. His Mission is still active among them.

During those exciting summers we who lived on the *Sunbeam* used to carry all manner of much-needed things to the islands and to the light stations. Sometimes our freight was curious enough. Once we took a cow to a new baby, hungry for milk. Our voyage was a rough one; and the poor cow was desperately seasick. Perhaps I would best not describe too realistically that memorable voyage with that most wretched of cows except to say that it will always be unforgettable!

So—I have happily known those boys and girls whose early lives as the children of lighthouse keepers were spent far away from the things which most boys and girls have always taken as a matter of course: schools, bicycles, shops, people, libraries, parties, and friends. And because they knew none of these things they were vastly different from you and me. What were they like? What human qualities are made from loneliness and isolation? What does the sea give one, its calms, its storms, the heavy fog which sometimes dims the air above it for weeks on end? What traits of character does one gain from the necessity of relying upon oneself for fun and for play, from the responsibility of caring, perhaps, for younger brothers and sisters, and from the need, at times, of helping to keep the lights always glowing for the safety of passing ships?

2

Lighthouse boys and girls, I early noted, possessed always certain qualities in common. In the first place, they were physically quick and agile. If you live on a small, rocky island, you learn very early to be quick and agile. The sea always surrounds you, your enemy as well as your friend; and you have to cope with all its moods. You must know the times of the rise and the fall of its tides; you learn to watch weather signs. As you scramble among the rocks which are your home, and play your games, you do both with the knowledge that waves may suddenly halt both the games and you. You grow careful to keep away from clefts and fissures into which you may fall. You learn when and how a boat can be safely launched and when it can't. And you know how to launch one, too.

"My little brother's still on ropes," a ten-year-old boy on a remote light station once said to me. "But next year when he's five, he'll be off them, and then he can run about with me."

I suppose the surprise in my face prompted his explanation.

"I mean he's tied up now so he can't fall into the big holes between the cliffs at the edge," he said. "We're all on ropes till we are four or five, or we might be drowned, you see."

He said this with the utmost ease as though drowning were a mere incident in human existence; and at the

124

same time he pointed toward the outside iron ladder of the light tower. There, sure enough, was his little brother securely tied to one of its rungs—"still on ropes," in his lighthouse language.

Such boys and girls are wary, too. They may not expect the worst, but they are ready for it. They learn not to take silly chances. They know that they are far away from a doctor and must rely upon their mother and her homely remedies for cuts and bruises, and even for worse. On one Maine island of perhaps three or four acres, which even boasted a few sturdy, windswept trees and a small pasture where some brave blueberries grew, I once found a boy of thirteen, who had broken his arm through stumbling on the steep, winding lighthouse stairs. A high wind and heavy sea had prevented his father from taking him to the mainland some six miles away to have his arm set; yet it had been bandaged tightly in the meantime by someone, probably his mother, and placed in a sling; and he seemed to look upon his accident only as the result of his own awkwardness and stupidity.

"My father says I ought to know them stairs by now," he said cheerfully. "He don't have too much sympathy for me, and I guess he's right."

The *Sunbeam*, which for many years has constantly

carried lighthouse dwellers to mainland doctors, wanted to carry him, also; but his father politely refused.

"I can get the motor boat off tomorrow," he said. "A few bits of pain won't hurt him any. They'll teach him to watch his step. He'll learn you can't go galli-vantin' around on lighthouse stairs."

Lighthouse boys and girls, as I have known them, are self-sufficient, observant, interested in all things about them. They are not really lonely, for they know no other life. Nor do they often feel deprived, since they have never experienced those pleasures which other children look upon as their normal and natural lot in life. Not having a host of friends to play with, they find substitutes along their shores, among their rocks. They know the habits of sea birds, where and how they build their nests, and are thrilled beyond words when they discover eggs and young. The tides are their great givers. Sometimes the sea washes up bright lobster buoys, odd bottles cast overboard by some vessel, round glass or cork floats of seines, every sort of shell. All these they gather with vast pride.

In the early autumn they are sure of sad excitement from the migrating birds which, attracted and dazzled by the light, dash themselves against the glass of the lantern and fall, dead or wounded, upon the rocks below. I have seen every sort of bird on Maine light stations: tiny ruby-throated hummingbirds on their long flight to South America, which now they will never see; thrushes, robins, every kind of swallow, sparrow, and warbler. If some of these have escaped death, they are tenderly cared for by the children who have found them, until they are able to fly away again; so that with all the sorrow which they bring every year to the light stations, they also now and then solicit care and affection which they are sure to receive from their excited foster parents.

Lighthouse boys and girls are uniformly capable, proud of what they can do. They early learn about the light which their fathers keep so that should he or his assistants, if he has them, be ill or injured, they themselves, like Abbie Burgess on Matinicus Rock, can step into the breach. They know the intricacies of the lantern, how it is cleaned and made ready to be lighted, how it must be tended all night long. They know how to handle oars, too; and not a few of them, in the years when I knew them, in addition to fishing for flounders and cunners whenever the sea allowed, set their own lobster traps in the water off their ledges and proudly supplied fresh sea-food for the family table.

A trip to the nearest mainland town meant, I early learned, the greatest possible occasion for them, one not often realized except in the summer months, but eagerly anticipated through all the winter storms. It meant to them strange sights and sounds; space, shops, a chance to spend carefully hoarded pennies; a chance to look upon churches and schools, horses, automobiles, many people, trees, and garden flowers. They might well feel shy and out of place in a mainland town; but even shyness was a small price to pay for such wonders as they would look upon.

Once I knew a little girl of seven on a remote Maine island who had never seen a horse, except in a picture. The dream of her life, however, was not to look upon a horse, but an elephant. Since she was so young, she had never been to the mainland twelve miles away; but her father had solemnly promised that he would take her on his next trip there.

"There might even be a circus," she said to me. "My mother went to a circus once when she was a little girl. She says that circuses travel about from town to town. They say there's always an elephant in a circus, swinging his trunk ahead of him. I would so love to see a real, live elephant! I might even buy some peanuts to give him."

128

3

In those years when I visited so many lighthouses I never ceased to be surprised over the many things which lighthouse children did not really know, things which their parents had told them about or which they had, perhaps, seen only in books. Like all children everywhere they loved to listen to stories; yet the telling of the most familiar stories was difficult, simply because they did not understand the things of which the stories were made. For example, the old, wonderful story of the boy Karl, who hid in the Nuremberg stove, was strange and mysterious to them.

The boys and girls at the particular light station where I told that story had never seen, even in pictures, any stove except the black, squat one on which their mother cooked; and it was almost impossible for them to imagine a great, tiled stove which reached to the ceiling and which was big enough to hide a good-sized boy. It was hard, too, to make them understand the depths of snow through which Karl walked. They knew snow, of course, and bitter cold; but on their island the snow never stayed, since the wind blew it away. The very idea of a snowdrift was incomprehensible to them, as was a sled, or a snow man, or a snowball fight. All these quite ordinary things were totally absent from their limited frame of reference.

They found many trees unimaginable, too. The thought of a vast forest, like that through which Hansel and Gretel wandered, was impossible for them to picture. If they knew any trees at all, they were windswept, crooked, solitary trees, likely at any hour to be torn up with their scanty roots and blown into the sea. Masses of trees which shut out the sun and extended for miles were as alien to them as were schoolrooms, big parties of laughing children, Christmas trees laden with lights and tinsel, swings, baseball games, snowshoes and skis, a daily newspaper.

Yet they all had their compensations: the sea gulls whom they tamed and fed; their daily surprises from the generous tides which washed their rocky shores; their closely knit companionship with brothers and sisters, or perhaps with the families of assistant keepers if their island were a fairly large one; the boats which they saw passing by; an infrequent visitor, if the sea allowed a landing; the bright feathers from some dead bird unknown to them. They loved the books which we brought to them, so full of things and pictures, strange and curious; and when we came the following summer with more books, the ones which we had left behind were tattered to bits from much turning of pages.

"I'm going to keep a light when I grow up," many lighthouse boys said to me. "I know already just how it's done. I don't need to learn any more."

I wonder if their dream has come true. I hope it has; yet the sad fact is that we don't need lighthouse keepers as we used to need them.

✣ VIII ✣

Going to School in a Lighthouse

ONE OF THE CHIEF PROBLEMS ALWAYS FACING
our keepers of lights has been the education of their
children; and this problem was especially urgent when
the salaries paid to keepers were very small and when
the nearest mainland towns with their schools were far
distant, or at least seemed far distant to men dependent
upon small boats and even more dependent upon
weather with its sudden changes. In the years before
1939, when, as we have seen, the Coast Guard assumed
responsibility for all United States light stations, our

135

lighthouses and the men who kept them were controlled by the Lighthouse Board until the year 1910, when this Board gave place to a similar organization known as the Lighthouse Service. Salaries, hardly more than nominal under the Lighthouse Board during the two centuries of its supervision, became, it is true, higher as the cost of living rose in the present century and the value of the dollar sank; and yet no keeper received wages sufficient to allow for the mainland education of his children—an expense which, of course, meant room and board, even though the schools themselves were free. It is true that certain allowances were granted to keepers for the education of their children; and yet it is equally true that these were never large enough to make the educational problem an easy one; and, of course, no amount of money, however generous, could make easier the matter of carrying and fetching, the taking of boys and girls over a rough sea, and any reliable promise that they could return home now and then, no matter how homesick they might be.

Another problem was added both to those of money and the weather. Many boys and girls who knew no other environment than that of remote islands did not take easily to a life away from that which they had always known. Much as they loved occasional trips to

the mainland with one or both of their parents to guide
and to guard them, they were, quite understandably,
shy and awkward when they were on their own in mainland schools. They were not only ill-prepared for their
studies; they found social life on the mainland unwel-
come and difficult. Their clothes might well be different
from those of mainland children; or they did not understand mainland games, or speech, or manners. They
were not used to living among many people; they even
missed silence and the sea. They did not want to leave
their few rocky acres, the life they had always known.
To many of them education was not so much an oppor-
tunity to be gratefully seized upon as it was a task to be
stolidly endured.

Those states with coastlines and, therefore, with
islands included in their areas were, in several cases,
considerate and even generous in their added financial
help to lighthouse keepers; and yet there was always the
almost insuperable problem raised by winds and storms,
and as well the added one of the happiness of the children themselves. The State of Maine, aware of these
difficulties, both financial and personal, and also keenly
aware of the many lighthouses off its long, indented,
dangerous shores began more than half a century ago
to take an active interest in the children on the light

137

stations. Wisely or unwisely (and there is perhaps something to be said in defense of both those adverbs), Maine decided to send a teacher to the lighthouses rather than to bring unwilling boys and girls to school in the nearest mainland town. If they wanted to come, or if they could be persuaded to do so, provision was gladly made for them; but for the very young and for those who could not fit at least fairly easily into a strange environment, a teacher was found who was adventuresome enough to fit herself into theirs. And such adjustment on the part of the teacher demanded a real sense of adventure, not to mention excellent health and a desire to be of service to others.

2

For many years I knew such a teacher very well, largely through the Maine Seacoast Mission, which from the beginning assumed a good part of the educational problem and was especially valuable for its carrying of the teacher from light to light. Of course, at its very best, lighthouse teaching was in many ways unsatisfactory; and yet it provided untold riches to the children on the lighthouse islands. The teacher whom I knew for

138

fully fifteen years was as brave as she was lively and attractive. Her stay at each light station where there were children of school age was usually not longer than two or three weeks; but often that time to the delight of her pupils was greatly prolonged because of high seas which prevented her departure to yet another school-room of her watery domain. Sometimes there was a full month of school. Once during an especially severe winter, a certain lighthouse, to its joy and to the envy of all other Maine stations, kept the teacher for six whole weeks!

The lighthouse teacher held her school sometimes in the keeper's house, more often in the large open room at the base of the tower; and she taught the same subjects which were taught in mainland schools: reading, which most lighthouse children had already learned from their mothers, arithmetic, American history, geography, and grammar. Grammar, she told me, was usually the most difficult of all subjects, since to most lighthouse children language was a necessity rather than an adornment, and its correctness hardly one of paramount importance to them. For the most part, however, she found her students quick and capable, vastly interested in the history of their country, only a tiny scrap of which they knew well, and always excited by the knowledge of far-off lands, which to them largely meant colored spaces on a map and which none of them ever so much as dreamed of seeing for themselves.

She told me that they, in their turn, taught her numberless things: what the skies foretold in terms of weather; the many things one could do for amusement and pleasure when there seemed to be nothing at all outside school hours; the rigs of passing vessels, whether they were seiners, or schooners, or mere lobster boats. They taught her, too, the secrets of taking things as they came, without grumbling and without fear; the acceptance of discomfort; the quiet, courageous understanding that one was ashamed to fuss too much over minor hurts and injuries; and always the unspoken and perhaps not fully understood responsibility which one must feel for another, whether for a younger child, a sick mother, the great light in the tower, or for sailors in their ships.

Accustomed to narrow, even cramped surroundings, lighthouse families must always see to it that everything had its own place, was kept there and nowhere else, that living quarters as well as the light tower were immaculate and shining, not only against the unannounced visits of government inspectors, but for the comfort and convenience of all.

School on lighthouse stations knew no free Saturdays. All days given to study were precious and far too brief. Sunday was the one day off; and on that day not only was everyone a bit cleaner than usual, but the lighthouse teacher was supposed to be able and willing to teach a Sunday school lesson and to hold some sort of simple religious service. Evenings were spent in reading aloud under kerosene lamps, with the keeper and his wife as eager listeners as were the children—evenings broken only by long climbings to the summit of the tower to be sure that all was well there.

The lighthouse teacher knew no summer holidays. She taught in one station or another for eleven months each year. February was usually her one month off duty, because February was likely to bring such storms and cold that to journey from light to light was always dangerous and sometimes impossible, even for so stout and manageable a boat as was the *Sunbeam*.

"The first thing I always do when I get home in February," the lighthouse teacher once told me, "is to throw away all the things I don't really need; and the next thing is to put in perfect order all I have left. Living on lighthouse stations has taught me that tidiness is not just a virtue, but that it's by far the easiest way to live."

3

One summer, around the year 1925, I taught for a month on a Maine light station, on an island of five or six acres, where one of our most important United States lights rears its great granite tower one hundred and twenty-two feet into the air. It was built in 1821; and it is still as strong as when it was first placed on its dangerous rocks. When I taught there, as a volunteer under the Seacoast Mission, there were six children, ranging in age from five to fourteen, three boys and three girls.

I shall never forget that singular experience. After the *Sunbeam* had left me with my few possessions, and I watched it steaming off until it was swallowed up by the far horizon and lost to sight, I thought I had never before known the feeling of utter loneliness which enveloped me like some heavy, suffocating gray blanket. That night, when I opened the window of my tiny, immaculate room in the keeper's house, heard the sea crashing on the rocks below, and saw the stars seemingly so near that I could reach up and pluck one out of the sky for companionship, I wondered if I had within me what it takes to live for even four days, let alone four weeks, in such isolation.

But in the morning, when from the kitchen below I

heard the familiar sound of an egg beater, the familiar sizzle of a hot frying pan, when I saw from my window my oldest pupil skillfully rowing his dory to the landing slip of the boat shed and casually jumping ashore with a string of fresh flounders, I decided that if I didn't have what it takes, everyone else on that island did, and that I'd better at least *pretend* that I was neither lonely nor scared.

It proved to be a wonderful month. My six pupils were eager not only to learn, but to teach. They taught me more than I have ever learned at any college or university in any country, in an equal space of time.

Some of the things I learned from them were of a practical nature: how to row a boat better and with less strain on one's back and arms by changing one's position, by standing now and again instead of constantly sitting; how to use one's hands as well as one's feet in scrambling among sharp rocks; how to mount one hundred and twenty winding stairs to the lantern room of the tower without getting dizzy or breathless; how to bait a hook so that the bait can't slip off in deep water; how to tie any number of intricate knots.

The other things they taught me are less easily listed and described. Perhaps the chief one was that loneliness is not the product of great stretches of empty sea, of empty skies, or of those filled with blazing stars or with streaming Northern Lights; but that it is rather the product of emptiness within oneself, of the failure to find thoughts by which to live, the inability to discover things to do both with one's hands and with one's mind.

My boys and girls on that remote island, alone as they were, were not really lonely. They had countless resources. They admired their parents as well as loved them. They were proud of their light, which was always protecting the ships at sea. Although they knew very little about their country, its size, its great and various extent, they felt that they were serving it, as indeed they were. They may not have recognized that they were thinking good and even noble thoughts, yet they were doing that very thing.

Their talent for inventing new games was limitless.

"Let's call this game *Whiz*," Arthur said one day. "It's to see who can get to the highest rock on this island with his hands tied behind his back. It's only for us over eight. No babies allowed. There's a prize, too, for the winner. It's two helpings for supper. Nobody else gets more than one. And it's going to be lobster, too."

We held our school in the rather bare room at the base of the light tower. There we had some chairs and improvised benches for desks; and there from nine in

144

the morning until four in the afternoon we worked over our books, which the Mission had left for us. We learned among other things that one doesn't say *hadn't ought*, but *ought not.*

"I'll try," Mary, who was eleven, would say, "but I don't think it matters much on this island what anybody says. Anyhow it hadn't ought to matter. We're just out here, all by ourselves, and nobody cares how we talk. It's much more important to keep our light burning, now ain't it? My father says *hadn't ought*, but he's a prime lightkeeper."

4

I think the one subject which really fascinated my lighthouse children during that month of August was *oranges.* I never see an orange today without thinking of them all: Arthur and Mary, Paul and Elsie, Roger and Millicent. Arthur and Roger are dead now. They went to war in 1941, in the United States Navy, of course, and they were killed in Sicily during the landings there. I have always hoped that perhaps they saw an orange tree before they died.

It was the orange tree rather than its round, golden balls of fruit which thrilled my six lighthouse children.

They could not understand how any tree could have blossoms and fruit on it at one and the same time. Of course, they believed the books which said so, for they had a deep regard, even reverence for books; and perhaps they believed me even more surely, for, to their amazement, I had seen orange trees both in California and in Spain. Our geography had a series of colored pictures; and one of these showed an orange tree with its waxen, shining leaves, its white flowers, and its golden globes of oranges. All six of them stared at this marvel every day; and all six demanded pauses between fractions and grammar so that I could tell them more about those incredible orange trees.

"I had an orange once," Millicent, who was the youngest, said. "The Mission brought it to me. I didn't ever want to eat it, only just to look at it and hold it in my hand."

"I've seen oranges on the mainland, in the stores there," Paul, who was fourteen, said, perhaps a bit importantly since, because he was never seasick and handled a boat well, he had gone often to the mainland. "They are piled up there in bins, hundreds of them; but they cost too much for us, my father always says. I don't suppose, though, I'll ever see a real orange tree."

"If you had only saved the seeds in your orange," I told Millicent, "and let them dry long enough, you might have planted one in a pot of earth. Then you would perhaps have had a tiny orange tree for yourself."

Arthur looked more than a little scornfully at me.

"Even if she had," he said, "I don't think it would have lived long away out here. Trees have to have sun and air; and if you once put them outside the door, the wind blows them away, or else a wave hits them and they die. You're just here in the summer, teacher. You don't know what it's like when the gales hit in winter."

"Anyhow, if I ever have another orange," Millicent said, "I shall try to plant a seed in a pot of earth."

"Is Spain a nice country?" Arthur asked me. "My father says that if we could just see far enough across the sea away out eastward, there would be Spain. Thousands of miles away, of course, but he says there it is, even if we can't see that far."

"He's right," I said. "It's there, way out beyond the horizon, with all its orange groves."

"What's a *grove*?" Elsie asked. "I ain't never heard of a grove."

"You mean you *haven't ever* heard of a grove," I said. "Remember we don't say *ain't*. A grove is a great many trees all together, and all with oranges on them. Yes, Spain *is* a nice country with hot sunshine nearly every day. The hot sunshine makes the orange trees grow so that all the oranges become big and yellow."

147

"I don't suppose I'll ever see Spain," Roger said, "if I keep a light like my father. And that's what I aim to do when I'm a man. But I just might see California if I could save enough money to go on a train away out there. Would the orange trees be just the same in California?"

"Just the same," I said. "And now we really must get back to our fractions and our grammar lesson. We've spent far too much time today on orange trees."

"No, we ain't, please, teacher," Mary said. "I had a dream last night about an orange tree. It was growing right here with all its flowers, too—right here among our rocks. And I reached up in my dream and picked an orange off whenever I had a mind to. It was a lovely dream."

"Silly!" Arthur said. "There couldn't be no orange tree away out here, not even in a dream."

Mary looked a bit crestfallen at her brother's words. But still, I could see, she was cherishing her lovely dream.

❖ IX ❖

The Keepers of the Lights

ONE OF THE MOST CHARACTERISTIC TRAITS OF
men who have kept the lighthouses of the world glowing through darkness and storm has been their conviction that they were an indispensable part of human
society, that they were serving their countries by their
difficult, dangerous, and lonely work. Their countries
quite reasonably have held the same conviction. Queen
Victoria acted well when she conferred a knighthood
on James Douglass, the builder of the fourth and the
present Eddystone tower; her Prime Minister, Mr. Glad-

stone, and her Parliament felt precisely as she did.

In our own country our earliest Presidents and our foremost statesmen have, one and all, left records of their deep interest in our lighthouses and in the men chosen to keep them. We have already seen how Alexander Hamilton, then Secretary of the United States Treasury, was responsible in 1794 for a lighthouse on Cape Hatteras. George Washington, as the first President of a new country, did not feel himself too important to be concerned with even the cost of necessary lighthouse ropes and chains. We still have records of this concern in his own handwriting. Thomas Jefferson was deeply anxious lest the tendency among many keepers to hand on their work to their sons should result in the appointment of unworthy men to such important posts. In the year 1806 he insisted that this custom be carefully scrutinized so that only the best men might be appointed to fill such necessary and responsible positions. If the sons of keepers were as brave and reliable as were their fathers, well and good; but if they were not, then they could not succeed their fathers as keepers.

It has been especially true in the United States that the keepers of our lights have tended to hand over their jobs to their sons, so that almost a dynasty of lightkeepers from father to son, even from grandfather to grandson, became the custom before the Coast Guard annexed the lighthouses to its service. It seemed only reasonable that boys brought up upon light stations, inured to isolation, familiar with all details of the work of lightkeeping, should follow after their fathers. I myself have known several Maine light stations where keepers have spoken proudly of the fact that they were the third, or the fourth, in line in a family of lightkeepers. Yet in order that such a custom, however reasonable, might not result in a poor choice of keepers, a tough Civil Service examination came to be required of all young men eager to take over the work of their fathers. This examination included not only the test of proving that candidates could read and write sufficiently well, but a stringent manual test to make certain that they were also skillful in the work of their hands.

2

Many qualities were, of course, necessary for a keeper to possess. In strictly physical terms he must be a man vigorous, dexterous, and skillful, not only in the knowledge of lighthouse routine, but in the handling of boats as well and in the care of them. If his light station were large enough to have a landing slip and a boat shed, he had to be capable in carpentry, since any high gale with its accompanying waves might in but a few hours completely demolish the boards of his slip and wreak havoc with his shed as well. He had also to be an expert in painting and whitewashing, completely at home on high and dangerous places; for at least once a year the ironwork around his lantern, rusted and corroded by fog and sea water, must be freshly painted, and his tower, if it were kept white as many towers were, must be whitewashed from tapering top to solid bottom. The accomplishment of such work often meant sitting in a basket or a sling many feet above the ground and moving oneself up and down, round and round, by ropes and pulleys. His winding iron staircase, a hundred or more steps in height, must receive each year its coat of fresh paint, and always in such a carefully managed way that it was never entirely useless to the tender of the lantern. The house in which he lived must likewise be kept in shining, immaculate order, floors painted or varnished, outside walls in perfect shape, panes of glass constantly replaced and always clean and clear. A lighthouse, in other words, was like the ships which it protected in that it must be kept in as perfect order as they were kept. Its keeper was never unprepared for the government Inspection Officers, who always took care to appear quite unannounced and whose sharp eyes missed nothing at all.

Not a few of these tasks fell upon the keeper's wife, who spent a large part of all her days in scrubbing and polishing her small rooms and who also helped in the tower. Brass presented a particular problem, since fog and salt water are adept in dulling the sheen of brass.

"If there's ever nothing else to do," a lightkeeper's wife once said to me, "there's always the brass to rub up again. Lighthouse inspectors always have a quick eye for brass. I suppose brass is going to be my enemy all my life, to be beaten every day I live."

3

The number of keepers on any light station has always varied, of course, with the size and the location of the station. Even today on the great Eddystone Light there are always three keepers in its lonely tower, although an electric lamp has taken the place of one lighted by oil and has, of course, greatly simplified the labor. There used to be long ago only two Eddystone keepers; but after the tragedy of the sudden death of one of these men in John Rudyerd's tower and the necessity for his companion to remain on duty (alone for a full month with the dead body of his assistant before any help could be sent to him), three men has been the Eddystone number, or really four to allow for one always to be on leave. On sizable islands like Petit Manan off the Maine coast there were, before 1939, both an assistant keeper and an engineer, whose chief job was the care of the fog siren; for on a light station so near the Bay of Fundy with its heavy fogs the whistle or wail of a siren all day, and often all night as well, was of equal importance with the streaming, revolving light.

All these men, whether alone or with but one family as they were on small stations, or with assistants and perhaps other families on large stations, must, of course, be men both of courage and of personal resources. In days before the telephone to the mainland, before radio, and years before television, such men, whether or not with wives and families, learned to depend upon themselves for pleasure and for recreation. Some of them were fishermen when the sea allowed such pastime, thus procuring food for their own tables or perhaps even selling their fish or lobsters to passing vessels, or to the nearest mainland settlement when the sea permitted them to carry their fish there. On certain stations that I have known a strip of white cloth blowing from the top of the tower meant fresh sea-food for sale; and the venturesome pilots of various craft would draw as near as possible to meet the keeper with his laden dory in order that they might purchase his wares.

Other light-keepers learned to do all manner of things. Some made themselves students of birds, gulls, terns, sandpipers, ospreys, eagles. Some enjoyed collecting stamps; or whittling out boats, and rigging them with twine and sails; or painting pictures, perhaps not good ones from the point of view of art, but very good for the cultivation of a man's eyes and imagination. I once knew several lightkeepers who braided and hooked rugs. I have in my home today a rug designed and hooked by the keeper of a light. It shows most realistically the surf beating against his island rocks; and I am told by those who presumably know about design and perspective that it is very well done. He told me when he gave it to me that it had taken most of his spare time during a severe winter. I could see that he felt vast pride in it as, indeed, he should have.

Trips to the mainland were necessary, at least once a month, not only for the purpose of getting food supplies and for gathering up mail, but for learning what was going on in the outside world. These meant for the keeper a welcome hour in some country store, talking with men who lived a far different life, gathering up precious nuggets of news to share with his few companions upon his return home, buying a bag of candies for the children before he took up his oars or hoisted his sail or cranked up his engine for the windy or foggy or wet voyage back to his tiny island or his waveswept ledge.

4

Children on light stations have always presented problems as well as pleasures, just as they themselves have known from their singular life deprivations as well as delights. Education has by no means been the only anxiety. Tough and strong as most lighthouse children have been from their very environment, the fear of illness or of accident has haunted their parents.

Some thirty years ago, on an isolated Maine island station with but one keeper, two children, a boy and a girl of ten and twelve years, were drowned. They had been overtaken by an unusually high tide while they were hunting for sea treasures in a deep fissure between two walls of rock. They were the only children of the keeper and his wife; and when the belated news, retarded by stormy weather, was finally known, great concern was felt for the parents, who, all thought, would now leave their light for the mainland or, at all events, for another and less dangerous station.

They did not leave. They stayed on for fifteen years longer, in spite of attractive inducements both from individuals on the mainland and from the Lighthouse Service itself. And perhaps no more true description of lightkeepers at their noblest could be given than to repeat what they said, not only about their own bitter sorrow, but about the tending of their light.

"Yes, of course, it's terrible lonesome, especially in dirty weather," the keeper said. "But we're used to lonesomeness. It's too many strange folks who would bother us. Besides, someone has to keep this light; and my wife and I think it's just our job in life. No one much knows about us away off here; but *we* know we're doing something important. If we were on the mainland, we'd just be looking out for ourselves the way most mainland folks do. We always wanted everything best for our children; and now we know they're getting better things than we could have given them. Maybe that would sound foolish to some folks; but when you're way out here with only God and what He's made for real steady company, you get to believing in Him and in what He has planned for us all. If my wife wanted to leave, I'd go, too, of course; but she wants to stay the same as I do."

"Yes, I want to stay, too," his wife said. "I'd never be important in a mainland town, or even necessary to anyone at all. But I'm really necessary out here to help my husband keep this light. Nobody don't need to worry about us. We like the life we chose for ourselves. It's the only way we have of being of use to our country; and we want to be of use to it by tending our light."

5

As readers will have noticed, most of the tenses used in this chapter are past tenses. That is because the old, voluntary keepers of the lights belong now to the past. They have become a part of our history; yet they should never be forgotten.

For more than two centuries they manned our lighthouses. They were seldom men of what we call "education." Few of them had gone beyond the common schools. Their spelling, as we know from the records which they kept, was often faulty; their grammar was often incorrect. Yet they were a noble breed of men, and of women, too; and their names deserve a high place not only in American history, but in the history of every land and of every age.

They were as bold and courageous as they were versatile and ingenious. Whatever they may have lacked in life, they held close the knowledge that they were contributing to human safety. They were proud and gallant men; and our world is a better place because of their lives and their dangerous, self-sacrificing, lonely labor. Let us never forget to do them honor!

Index

Index

The Author

Few authors with such a large and devoted reading public as Mary Ellen Chase have received such widespread critical acclaim as well. A scholar as well as a writer of fiction and nonfiction, Miss Chase was for many years Professor of English Literature at Smith College. Such books as *Windswept, Mary Peters, The White Gate, The Edge of Darkness, The Lovely Ambition, The Psalms for the Common Reader* and *The Prophets for the Common Reader* have assured her a place as one of the United States' most widely respected adult authors, while her recent children's books, *Victoria: A Pig in a Pram, Richard Mansfield,* and *Dolly Moses,* all warm and humorous accounts of her childhood in Maine, have won her new readers from the younger generation.

Born in Blue Hill, Maine, Miss Chase earned her B.A. at

the University of Maine and her M.A. and Ph.D. at the University of Minnesota. She was a member of the English Department at Minnesota for eight years, after which time she returned to New England to join the faculty of Smith College.

Mary Ellen Chase holds honorary degrees from Northeastern University, Bowdoin, Smith, Wilson, and Goucher colleges. Her stories and reviews have appeared in such publications as *The New York Times,* the New York *Herald-Tribune,* the *Atlantic Monthly* and the *Yale Review.* She lives in Northampton, Massachusetts.

The Artist

Erwin Schachner, an Austrian by birth, left Vienna in 1938 and lived in France before coming to the United States in 1940. He graduated from the Philadelphia Museum School and attended Pratt Institute.

Mr. Schachner's woodcuts and linoleum cuts have been exhibited both in Philadelphia and New York. In addition, he has worked in the fields of advertising, printing, and magazine illustration. His book illustrations have covered such varied subjects as the history of medicine, life in early England, and the first Christmas.

He and his wife, who is a radio information specialist for the Voice of America, live in New York City.